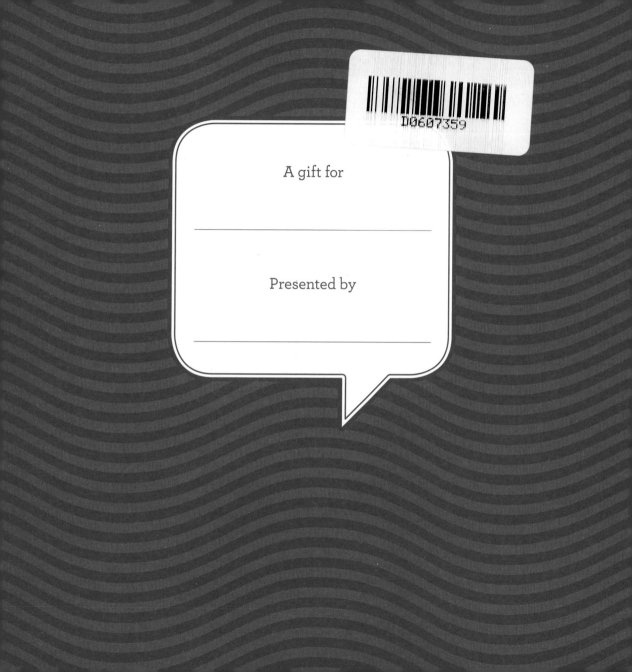

A gift for

_____

Presented by

_____

QUOTABLE QUOTES

Reader's
Digest

QUOTABLE QUOTES

ALL NEW WIT & WISDOM FROM THE GREATEST MINDS OF OUR TIME

Illustrations by John Kascht

The Reader's Digest Association, Inc.
New York, NY / Montreal

A READER'S DIGEST BOOK

The Reader's Digest Association, Inc. © 2013

Illustrations © John Kascht

All rights reserved. Unauthorized reproduction,
in any manner, is prohibited.

Reader's Digest is a registered trademark of
The Reader's Digest Association, Inc.

Library of Congress Cataloging in Publication Data

Quotable quotes : wit and wisdom from the greatest minds
of our time / editors of Reader's digest.
     p. cm.
  Includes bibliographical references and index.
   ISBN 978-1-62145-004-7 (alk. paper) — ISBN 978-1-62145-020-7
(e-pub) — ISBN 978-1-62145-019-1 (adobe)
  1. Quotations, English. I. Reader's Digest Association.
  PN6083.Q85 2012
  081—dc23

2012027574

ISBN 978-1-62145-004-7

We are committed to both the quality of our products and the service
we provide to our customers. We value your comments,
so please feel free to contact us.

The Reader's Digest Association, Inc.
Adult Trade Publishing
44 South Broadway
White Plains, NY 10601

For more Reader's Digest products and information,
visit our website:
www.rd.com

Printed in China

1 3 5 7 9 10 8 6 4 2

CONTENTS

"A word after a word after a word is power."

—MARGARET ATWOOD

Quotable Quotes are a well-loved tradition at *Reader's Digest*. Since they were introduced in 1933, they have represented what we do best: curate and condense. These quotes embody that undertaking by encapsulating in just a few words the thoughts, ideals, morals, and observations of truly great minds.

Through the years, we have continued to collect the most outstanding words by the people who shape the world. This book features our hand-picked favorites from the twenty-first century—quotes that succeed in capturing the zeitgeist of our age in sentiments that are themselves timeless—as well as adages from history that no volume of quotes would be complete without.

Gathered from speeches, magazines, television, online sources, and books by celebrities, scientists, business leaders, celebrities, politicians, and journalists, this is an expansive compendium of modern thought. These gems can both inspire your day-to-day life and provide you with the perfect words for all occasions. Whether you are putting together a wedding speech or a cover note, a love letter or courtroom remarks, a protest rally or an election campaign, our special features deliver an assortment of sentiments to illuminate your message.

In this era of technology, a time when communication races past us from around the globe, it is up to the curators to capture the words worth saving from the torrents of information. This is why we are proud to present Quotable Tweets. Culled from the Twitter feeds of some of the most recognizable names in our culture, these Quotable Tweets represent a new age where a dialogue between all people is possible.

This book aims to give you the greatest insights into our world from a wide range of views—from the left and right, the serious and humorous, the artistic and practical. We hope you enjoy this eclectic look at life and learn something about yourself and the people around you.

L. Vaccariello

Liz Vaccariello

Editor-in-Chief, *Reader's Digest*

> "I'm not a businessman.
> I'm a business, man."
>
> —JAY-Z

MAKING IT

Though we author our own destinies, we find inspiration in the success stories of others. By listening to the wisdom they have accrued, we can build the next steps into the future.

Success

Do or do not. There is no try.

—YODA

"

Don't just stand there; make something happen.

—LEE IACOCCA

"

Every success is usually an admission ticket
to a new set of decisions.

—HENRY KISSINGER

"

The key to success?
Work hard, stay focused and marry a Kennedy.

—ARNOLD SCHWARZENEGGER

"

Success is a lot like a bright, white tuxedo. You feel
terrific when you get it, but then you're desperately
afraid of getting it dirty, of spoiling it in any way.

—CONAN O'BRIEN

"

You only have to do a very few things right in your
life—so long as you don't do too many things wrong.

—WARREN BUFFETT

Anybody who's really successful has doubts.

—JERRY BRUCKHEIMER

"

There's a ball. There's a hoop. You put the ball
through the hoop. That's success.

—KAREEM ABDUL-JABBAR

"

Success is falling nine times and getting up ten.

—JON BON JOVI

"

Success is more permanent when you achieve
it without destroying your principles.

—WALTER CRONKITE

"

If you want to be successful, just meditate, man.
God will tell you what people need.

—CARLOS SANTANA

"

There is no point at which you can say, "Well, I'm
successful now. I might as well take a nap."

—CARRIE FISHER

"

Winning depends on where you put your priorities.
It's usually best to put them over the fence.

—JASON GIAMBI

If you're willing to fail interestingly, you tend
to succeed interestingly.

—EDWARD ALBEE

66

Celebrate what you've accomplished, but raise the bar
a little higher each time you succeed.

—MIA HAMM

66

To succeed in life, you need three things: a wishbone,
a backbone and a funnybone.

—REBA MCENTIRE

"Success is a lousy teacher.
It seduces people into
thinking they can't lose."

—BILL GATES

You cannot be really first-rate at your work
if your work is all you are.

—ANNA QUINDLEN

❝

Inside of a ring or out, ain't nothing wrong with going
down. It's staying down that's wrong.

—MUHAMMAD ALI

❝

There is no downside to winning.
It feels forever fabulous.

—PAT CONROY

❝

The person who knows "how" will always have a job.
The person who knows "why" will always be his boss.

—DIANE RAVITCH

Failure

The best of us must sometimes eat our words.
—J.K. ROWLING

"

Be bold. If you're going to make an error, make a doozy.
—BILLIE JEAN KING

"

An inventor fails 999 times, and if he succeeds once,
he's in. He treats his failures simply as practice shots.
—CHARLES KETTERING

"

Failure is just another way to learn
how to do something right.
—MARIAN WRIGHT EDELMAN

"

Failure is God's way of saying, "Excuse me,
you're moving in the wrong direction."
—OPRAH

"

Winning may not be everything,
but losing has little to recommend it.
—DIANNE FEINSTEIN

"

When you win, say nothing. When you lose, say less.
—PAUL BROWN

Whoever said "It's not whether you win or lose
that counts" probably lost.

—MARTINA NAVRATILOVA

"

Second Place is just the first place loser.

—DALE EARNHARDT

"

I've missed more than 9,000 shots.
I've lost almost 300 games. I've failed over and over
again in my life. And that is why I succeed.

—MICHAEL JORDAN

Talent

....

Genius is immediate, but talent takes time.

—JANET FLANNER

"

Talent is only a starting point.

—IRVING BERLIN

"

We are all born with a grab bag of gifts and gaps.
Identify your true talents, then find out how to use
them to make money.

—BILL O'REILLY

Some are born great, some achieve greatness
and some hire PR officers.
—DANIEL J. BOORSTIN

"

Just because someone has fancy sneakers
doesn't mean they can run faster.
—JON BON JOVI

"

You have to be first, different, or great.
If you're one of them, you may make it.
—LORETTA LYNN

"

Persistence trumps talent and looks every time.
—AARON BROWN

"A peacock that rests
on his feathers is just
another turkey."

—DOLLY PARTON

16

Hire character. Train skill.

—PETER SCHUTZ

Work for It

Amateurs wait for inspiration.
The rest of us just get up and go to work.

—CHUCK CLOSE

‘‘

There's nothing you've ever been successful
at that you didn't work on every day.

—WILL SMITH

‘‘

I'd rather work with someone who's good
at their job but doesn't like me, than someone
who likes me but is a ninny.

—SAM DONALDSON

THE PERFECT WORDS FOR
Breaking Bad News

You never conquer a mountain. You stand
on the summit a few moments; then the
wind blows your footprints away.

—ARLENE BLUM

"

Success and failure. We think of them as opposites,
but they're really not. They're companions—
the hero and the sidekick.

—LAURENCE SHAMES

"

Success covers a multitude of blunders.

—GEORGE BERNARD SHAW

"

Failure is the condiment that gives success its flavor.

—TRUMAN CAPOTE

"

It takes as much courage to have tried and failed
as it does to have tried and succeeded.

—ANNE MORROW LINDBERGH

"

Failure is an event, never a person.

—WILLIAM D. BROWN

It isn't failing that spells one's downfall;
it's running away, giving up.

—MICHEL GRECO

"

Being defeated is often a temporary condition.
Giving up is what makes it permanent.

—MARILYN VOS SAVANT

"

Success is not forever, and failure's not fatal.

—DON SHULA WITH KEN BLANCHARD

"

Oh, the difference between nearly right
and exactly right.

—HORACE J. BROWN

"

If you're not failing now and again,
it's a sign you're playing it safe.

—WOODY ALLEN

"

I'd rather be a failure at
something I enjoy than a
success at something I hate.

—GEORGE BURNS

QUOTABLE TWEETS

The world is our office.

@kanyewest

If you don't keep pushing the limits, you wake up one day and you're the "center square to block."

—ROBIN WILLIAMS

"

The talk you hear about adapting to change is not only stupid, it's dangerous. The only way you can manage change is to create it.

—PETER DRUCKER

"

Assume any career moves you make won't go smoothly. They won't. But don't look back.

—ANDY GROVE

Practice

I don't know if I practiced more than anybody, but I sure practiced enough. I still wonder if somebody—somewhere—was practicing more than me.

—LARRY BIRD

Practice is a means of inviting the perfection desired.
—MARTHA GRAHAM

One day of practice is like one day of clean living.
It doesn't do you any good.
—ABE LEMONS

If I've learned nothing else, it's that time and
practice equal achievement.
—ANDRE AGASSI

Good, better, best. Never let it rest. Until your
good is better and your better is best.
—TIM DUNCAN

In theory there is no difference between theory
and practice. In practice there is.
—YOGI BERRA

Practice does not make perfect.
Only perfect practice makes perfect.
—VINCE LOMBARDI

Champions keep playing until they get it right.
—BILLIE JEAN KING

The Right Attitude

Do not allow people to dim your shine because they are blinded. Tell them to put on some sunglasses.

—LADY GAGA

"

Fearlessness is the mother of reinvention.

—ARIANNA HUFFINGTON

"

If you have the choice between humble and cocky, go with cocky. There's always time to be humble later, once you've been proven horrendously, irrevocably wrong.

—KINKY FRIEDMAN

"

It is our responsibilities, not ourselves, that we should take seriously.

—PETER USTINOV

"

When you're out of willpower, you can call on stubbornness.

—HENRI MATISSE

"

When in doubt, look intelligent.

—GARRISON KEILLOR

I go into every game thinking I'm going to be
the hero. I have to, or I wouldn't enjoy it.

—DEREK JETER

"

If you make every game a life-and-death
proposition, you're going to have problems.
For one thing, you'll be dead a lot.

—DEAN SMITH

"

One of the secrets of life is to make stepping
stones out of stumbling blocks.

—JACK PENN

"

I know for sure that what we dwell
on is who we become.

—OPRAH

QUOTABLE TWEETS

@Tawni3469 Here is what is important.
As women we need to support one another not tear
each other down. Let's lift each other up.

@SuzeOrmanShow

23

Money

What's money? A man is a success if he
gets up in the morning and goes to bed at night
and in between does what he wants to do.

—BOB DYLAN

"

It's better to do nothing with your money
than something you don't understand.

—SUZE ORMAN

"

I don't care how much money you have,
free stuff is always a good thing.

—QUEEN LATIFAH

"

They say everybody gets 15 minutes. I hope I'm just
inside the first minute and the next 14 go really slow.

—TERRENCE HOWARD

🐦 QUOTABLE TWEETS

The greatest commodity to own is land. It is finite.
God is not making any more of it.

@realDonaldTrump

Money was never a big motivation for me,
except as a way to keep score. The real excitement
is playing the game.

—DONALD TRUMP

Do not hire a man who does your work for money,
but him who does it for love of it.

—HENRY DAVID THOREAU

The only foolproof path to wealth is inheritance.

—TOM AND DAVID GARDNER

Think Big

The greatest dreams are always unrealistic.

—WILL SMITH

Reach for the stars, even if you
have to stand on a cactus.

—SUSAN LONGACRE

Don't listen to those who say you're taking
too big a chance. [If he had], Michelangelo
would have painted the Sistine floor.

—NEIL SIMON

THE PERFECT WORDS FOR
Cover Letters

Real success is finding your lifework in
the work that you love.
—DAVID MCCULLOUGH

"

The work praises the man.
—IRISH PROVERB

"

Just as there are no little people or unimportant
lives, there is no insignificant work.
—ELENA BONNER

"

One of the greatest sources of energy
is pride in what you are doing.
—UNKNOWN

"

The more I want to get something done,
the less I call it work.
—RICHARD BACH

"

Pleasure in the job puts perfection in the work.
—ARISTOTLE

Why not go out on a limb? Isn't that where the fruit is?

—FRANK SCULLY

"

My father always told me, "Find a job you love
and you'll never have to work a day in your life."

—JIM FOX

"

What isn't tried won't work.

—CLAUDE MCDONALD

"

What would life be if we had no
courage to attempt anything?

—VINCENT VAN GOGH

"

You do your best work if you do a
job that makes you happy.

—BOB ROSS

"

Genius begins great works; labor
alone finishes them.

—JOSEPH JOUBERT

🐦 QUOTABLE TWEETS

I finally made it home from a very trying week.
It reminds me of when my mother used to say
"if u think u seen it all just keep on living."

@IAMJHUD (Jennifer Hudson)

It's a whole lot more satisfying to reach for the stars,
even if you end up landing only on the moon.

—KERMIT THE FROG

"

It is often easier to make progress on mega-ambitious
dreams. Since no one else is crazy enough to do it,
you have little competition.

—LARRY PAGE

"

In order to be big, you have to think big.
If you think small, you're going to be small.

—EMERIL LAGASSE

"

Anything's possible if you've got enough nerve.

—J.K. ROWLING

"

Have great, secret, big, fat hopes for yourself.

—GLORIA VANDERBILT

There's nothing like biting off more than you can chew, and then chewing anyway.

—MARK BURNETT

Motivation

Start by starting.

—MERYL STREEP

"

It's hard to lead a cavalry charge if you think you look funny on a horse.

—ADLAI STEVENSON

"

Treat a person as he is, and he will remain as he is. Treat him as he could be, and he will become what he should be.

—JIMMY JOHNSON

"

No pressure, no diamonds.

—MARY CASE

"

To be a champion, you have to believe in yourself when nobody else will.

—SUGAR RAY ROBINSON

You'll never achieve 100 percent if 99 percent is okay.

—WILL SMITH

"

As I like to say, take the shot, even
if your knees are shaking.

—ROBIN ROBERTS

"

Great works are performed not by
strength, but perseverance.

—DR. SAMUEL JOHNSON

Education

The whole purpose of education is
to turn mirrors into windows.

—SYDNEY J. HARRIS

"

Education is what survives when what
has been learnt has been forgotten.

—B. F. SKINNER

"

[Learning] is the only thing which the mind
can never exhaust . . . never fear . . . and
never dream of regretting.

—T. H. WHITE

I think sleeping was my problem in school.
If school had started at four in the afternoon,
I'd be a college graduate today.

—GEORGE FOREMAN

"

Education's purpose is to replace an
empty mind with an open one.

—MALCOLM FORBES

"

Education is a progressive
discovery of our own ignorance.

—WILL DURANT

"Education is when
you read the fine print.
Experience is what
you get if you don't."

—PETE SEEGER

The mind is not a vessel that needs filling
but wood that needs igniting.

—PLUTARCH

"

That is what learning is. You suddenly
understand something you've understood
all your life but in a new way.

—DORIS LESSING

"

It's not just great teachers that shape your life.
Sometimes it's the absence of great teachers . . .
Being ignored can be just as good for
a person as being lauded.

—JULIA ROBERTS

"

When they said to you at graduation, "Follow your
dream," did anybody say you have to wake up first?

—BILL COSBY

🐦 QUOTABLE TWEETS

Students deserve great teachers. And teachers
deserve the support they need to become great.

@BillGates

Stress

Stress is your body's way of saying you haven't worked enough unpaid overtime.

—SCOTT ADAMS

"

Stress is an ignorant state. It believes that everything is an emergency.

—NATALIE GOLDBERG

"

Wringing your hands only stops you from rolling up your sleeves.

—JAMES ROLLINS

"

Stress should be a powerful driving force, not an obstacle.

—BILL PHILLIPS

"

Stress is nothing more than a socially acceptable form of mental illness.

—RICHARD CARLSON

"

Maturity is achieved when a person accepts life as full of tension.

—JOSHUA L. LIEBMAN

The Best Graduation Speeches

You can't connect the dots looking forward;
you can only connect them looking backward.
So you have to trust that the dots will somehow
connect. You have to trust in something—
your gut, destiny, life, karma.

—STEVE JOBS

"

I was a loser in high school. . . . And I'm here
to tell my fellow dweebs and losers that
your day will come. High school is not the
final word on you. There is hope.

—DOUG MARLETTE

"

How will your experience pave the way for a
new voice in America? I hope it will take you
out these doors, out into the open air. You will
breathe it in your lungs and say, "From now on,
this life will be what I stand for . . . Move over—
this is my story now."

—JODIE FOSTER

Getting up in the morning and having work
you love is what makes life different for people.
If you get into a position where you don't
love what you're doing, get off it.

—BOB WOODWARD

❝

The really important kind of freedom involves
attention and awareness and discipline, and being
able truly to care about other people and to
sacrifice for them over and over in myriad
petty, unsexy ways every day.

—DAVID FOSTER WALLACE

❝

The unfortunate, truly exciting thing about your life
is that there is no core curriculum. . . . So don't worry
about your grade or the results or success. Success
is defined in myriad ways, and you will find it,
and people will no longer be grading you.

—JON STEWART

❝

Education and the warm heart—if you combine these two,
then your education, your knowledge, will be construc-
tive. You are yourself then becoming a happy person.

—THE DALAI LAMA

"There's an old saying about those who forget history. I don't remember it, but it's good."

—STEPHEN COLBERT

AMERICA THE BEAUTIFUL

History is often written by the winners, but the records of what was said reflect the truth more closely. From politicians, protestors, and patriots, the spirit of our time is collected in the words by which we remember our leaders.

America

America is a vast conspiracy to make you happy.
—JOHN UPDIKE

"

America is not just a country. It's an idea.
—BONO

"

America is not perfect, but it's much better
than anywhere else in the world.
—CATHERINE ZETA-JONES

"

I think the most un-American thing you
can say is "You can't say that."
—GARRISON KEILLOR

"

America is so vast that almost everything
said about it is likely to be true, and the opposite
is probably equally true.
—JAMES T. FARRELL

"

Anyone who believes the competitive spirit in
America is dead has never been in a supermarket
when the cashier opens another checkout line.
—ANN LANDERS

Poker is to cards and games what jazz is to music.
It's this great American thing, born and bred here.
We dig it because everybody can play.

—STEVE LIPSCOMB

"

What is the essence of our America? Finding and
maintaining that perfect, delicate balance
between freedom "to" and freedom "from."

—MARILYN VOS SAVANT

"

You don't have to be old in America to say
of a world you lived in, "That world is gone."

—PEGGY NOONAN

"

Whoever wants to know the heart and mind
of America had better learn baseball.

—JACQUES BARZUN

"

The American dream is not over.
America is an adventure.

—THEODORE WHITE

"

America did not invent human rights.
In a very real sense, it is the other way around.
Human rights invented America.

—JIMMY CARTER

America is a place where Jewish merchants sell
Zen love beads to agnostics for Christmas.

—JOHN BURTON BRIMER

"

The things that have made America great are being
subverted for the things that make Americans rich.

—LOU ERICKSON

"

In America nobody says you have to keep the
circumstances somebody else gives you.

—AMY TAN

"

What's right with America is a willingness
to discuss what's wrong with America.

—HARRY C. BAUER

"

Being American is not a matter of birth. We must
practice it every day, lest we become something else.

—MALCOLM WALLOP

"

America is a tune. It must be sung together.

—GERALD STANLEY LEE

"

If there is anything that is important to America,
it is that you are not a prisoner of the past.

—DAVID HALBERSTAM

> "One of the fondest expressions around is that we can't be the world's policeman. But guess who gets called when suddenly someone needs a cop."
> —GEN. COLIN POWELL

Government

To lodge all power in one party and keep it there is to insure bad government.
—MARK TWAIN

❝

What Washington needs is adult supervision.
—BARACK OBAMA

❝

You don't pay taxes—they take taxes.
—CHRIS ROCK

A simple way to take the measure of a country is to look at how many want in . . . and how many want out.

—TONY BLAIR

"

Governing a large country is like frying a small fish. You spoil it with too much poking.

—LAO-TZU

"

A little government and a little luck are necessary in life, but only a fool trusts either of them.

—P. J. O'ROURKE

"

Everybody wants to eat at the government's table, but nobody wants to do the dishes.

—WERNER FINCK

"

Government can't give us anything without depriving us of something else.

—HENRY HAZLITT

"

When government accepts responsibility for people, then people no longer take responsibility for themselves.

—GEORGE PATAKI

Politics

Politics is the only business where doing nothing other than making the other guy look bad is an acceptable outcome.

—MARK WARNER

"

I looked up the word politics in the dictionary. It's actually a combination of two words: poli, which means many, and tics, which means bloodsuckers.

—JAY LENO

"

Ideas are great arrows, but there has to be a bow. And politics is the bow of idealism.

—BILL MOYERS

"

Everybody knows politics is a contact sport.

—BARACK OBAMA

"

Washington, D.C., is to lying what Wisconsin is to cheese.

—DENNIS MILLER

"

It's in the democratic citizen's nature to be like a leaf that doesn't believe in the tree it's part of.

—DAVID FOSTER WALLACE

THE PERFECT WORDS FOR
Protest Campaigns

There may be times when we are powerless
to prevent injustice, but there must never
be a time when we fail to protest.

—ELIE WIESEL

"

What is morally wrong cannot be politically right.

—WILLIAM GLADSTONE

"

To sin by silence when they should protest
makes cowards of men.

—ABRAHAM LINCOLN

"

A small body of determined spirits fired
by an unquenchable faith in their mission can
alter the course of history.

—MAHATMA GANDHI

"

You're not supposed to be so blind with patriotism
that you can't face reality. Wrong is wrong,
no matter who does it or who says it.

—MALCOLM X

You have the right to remain silent,
but I don't recommend it.

—PROTEST SIGN

"

Disobedience is the true foundation of liberty.
The obedient must be slaves.

—HENRY DAVID THOREAU

"

Never do anything against conscience
even if the state demands it.

—ALBERT EINSTEIN

"

As long as the world shall
last there will be wrongs, and
if no man objected and no man
rebelled, those wrongs
would last forever.

—CLARENCE DARROW

"

Man is not free unless government
is limited.

—RONALD REAGAN

"Take it from me— elections matter."

—AL GORE

Politics is the art of looking for trouble,
finding it everywhere, diagnosing it incorrectly,
and applying the wrong remedies.

—GROUCHO MARX

"

I'm older than dirt, I've got more scars
than Frankenstein, but I've learned
a few things along the way.

—JOHN MCCAIN

"

Where you stand should not depend on where you sit.

—JANE BRYANT QUINN

46

Elections

You campaign in poetry; you govern in prose.

—MARIO CUOMO

An election is coming. Universal peace
is declared, and the foxes have a sincere interest
in prolonging the lives of the poultry.

—GEORGE ELIOT

Do you ever get the feeling that the only reason we
have elections is to find out if the polls were right?

—ROBERT ORBEN

We pick politicians by how they look on TV
and Miss America on where she stands on
the issues. Isn't that a little backwards?

—JAY LENO

🐦 QUOTABLE TWEETS

Elections are when you have to make a choice.
Perfection not often attainable!

@rupertmurdoch

THE PERFECT WORDS FOR

Election Speeches

Change starts when someone sees the next step.
—WILLIAM DRAYTON

"

No person can be a great leader unless he takes
genuine joy in the successes of those under him.
—W. A. NANCE

"

Determine that the thing can and shall be
done, and then we shall find the way.
—ABRAHAM LINCOLN

"

Action may not always be happiness,
but there is no happiness without action.
—BENJAMIN DISRAELI

"

All glory comes from daring to begin.
—EUGENE F. WARE

"

It is easy to sit up and take notice.
What is difficult is getting up
and taking action.
—AL BATT

Anyone can hold the helm when the sea is calm.

—PUBLILIUS SYRUS

"

Well done is better than well said.

—BENJAMIN FRANKLIN

"

Change will not come if we wait for some other person or some other time. We are the ones we've been waiting for. We are the change that we seek.

—BARACK OBAMA

"

Dig the well before you are thirsty.

—CHINESE PROVERB

"

Not everything that is faced can be changed.
But nothing can be changed until it is faced.

—JAMES BALDWIN

"

Nothing great was ever achieved without enthusiasm.

—RALPH WALDO EMERSON

"

The most prominent place in hell is reserved for those who are neutral on the great issues of life.

—REV. BILLY GRAHAM

News

I wanted to see what was going on in the world.
I sometimes think I overwished.
—TOM BROKAW

"

Journalism has become a sort of competitive
screeching: What is trivial but noisy and
immediate takes precedence over important
matters that develop over time.
—TED KOPPEL

"News used to hold itself
to a higher plane, and
slowly it has dissolved
into, well, me."

—JON STEWART

50

Politicians who complain about the media are
like sailors who complain about the sea.

—ENOCH POWELL

History

Each time history repeats itself, the price goes up.

—RONALD WRIGHT

"

Well-behaved women never make history.

—MARIA SHRIVER

"

The past is a source of knowledge, and
the future is a source of hope. Love of the
past implies faith in the future.

—STEPHEN AMBROSE

"

Live out of your imagination, not your history.

—STEPHEN R. COVEY

"

Hindsight. It's like foresight without a future.

—KEVIN KLINE

QUOTABLE TWEETS

In a thousand years, archaeologists will dig up tanning beds and think we fried people as punishment.

@oliviawilde

Leadership

Great leaders are almost always great simplifiers.

—GEN. COLIN POWELL

"

A leader is one who, out of madness or goodness, volunteers to take upon himself the woe of the people. There are few men so foolish, hence the erratic quality of leadership.

—JOHN UPDIKE

"

Being powerful is like being a lady. If you have to tell people you are, you aren't.

—MARGARET THATCHER

"

Power is nothing unless you can turn it into influence.

—CONDOLEEZZA RICE

Good leadership requires you to surround yourself
with people of diverse perspectives who can disagree
with you without fear of retaliation.

—DORIS KEARNS GOODWIN

"

You have to have a vision. It's got to be
a vision you articulate clearly and forcefully.
You can't blow an uncertain trumpet.

—REV. THEODORE HESBURGH

"

Most people can bear adversity. But if you wish
to know what a man really is, give him power.

—ROBERT G. INGERSOLL

"

A leader takes people where they want to go.
A great leader takes people where they
don't necessarily want to go, but ought to be.

—ROSALYN CARTER

"

The day people stop bringing you their problems
is the day you have stopped leading them.

—GEN. COLIN POWELL

"

Leaders don't create followers,
they create more leaders.

—TOM PETERS

> **🐦 QUOTABLE TWEETS**
>
> True leadership is when you are willing to risk your power and voice so that ALL of ours can be heard.
>
> @jtimberlake

Leaders inspire. They aren't assigned leadership. They command it.

—DR. PHIL MCGRAW

Change

If you want to make enemies, try to change something.

—WOODROW WILSON

"

My parents told me, "Finish your dinner. People in China and India are starving." I tell my daughters, "Finish your homework. People in India and China are starving for your job."

—THOMAS FRIEDMAN

"

The main dangers in this life are the people who want to change everything . . . or nothing.

—LADY ASTOR

Never doubt that a small group of thoughtful, committed citizens can change the world. Indeed, it is the only thing that ever has.

—MARGARET MEAD

"

Our dilemma is that we hate change and love it at the same time; what we really want is for things to remain the same but get better.

—SYDNEY J. HARRIS

"A woman wasn't supposed to have a career. Today I'm convinced that there will be a woman President in my lifetime."

—SHERRY LANSING

THE PERFECT WORDS FOR

Open Court

A great many people in this country are worried about law-and-order. And a great many people are worried about justice. But one thing is certain: you cannot have either until you have both.

—RAMSEY CLARK

"

Justice is the insurance we have on our lives, and obedience is the premium we pay for it.

—WILLIAM PENN

"

That old law about "an eye for an eye" leaves everybody blind.

—REV. MARTIN LUTHER KING, JR.

"

Injustice is relatively easy to bear; what stings is justice.

—H. L. MENCKEN

"

The worst form of injustice is pretended justice.

—PLATO

"

In matters of truth and justice, there is no difference between large and small problems, for issues concerning the treatment of people are all the same.

—ALBERT EINSTEIN

"

It's every man's business to see justice done.

—SIR ARTHUR CONAN DOYLE

"

I would uphold the law if for no other reason but to protect myself.

—THOMAS MORE

"

It is better to risk saving a guilty man than to condemn an innocent one.

—VOLTAIRE

"

Injustice alone can shake down the pillars of the skies, and restore the reign of Chaos and Night.

—HORACE MANN

"

Defending the truth is not something one does out of a sense of duty or to allay guilt complexes, but is a reward in itself.

—SIMONE DE BEAUVOIR

Worrying is less work than doing something
to fix the worry. Everybody wants to save the earth;
nobody wants to help Mom with the dishes.

—P. J. O'ROURKE

"

If you don't like change, you're going
to like irrelevance even less.

—GEN. ERIC SHINSEKI

Ideas & Ideals

It's one thing to feel that you are on the right path, but
it's another to think that yours is the only path.

—PAULO COELHO

"

Injustice anywhere is a threat to justice everywhere.

—REV. MARTIN LUTHER KING, JR.

A bookstore is one of the only pieces of evidence
we have that people are still thinking.

—JERRY SEINFELD

"

Curious learning not only makes unpleasant
things less unpleasant but also makes pleasant
things more pleasant.

—BERTRAND RUSSELL

"

When a generation talks just to itself, it becomes
more filled with folly than it might have otherwise.

—STEWART BRAND

"

I think everybody has a right to happiness
and freedom and security and health care
and education and guitar lessons.

—BONNIE RAITT

🐦 QUOTABLE TWEETS

Let's get rid of the suffering and bring real
peace, which is not just the absence of war,
but the absence of all negativity.

@DAVID_LYNCH

Being President

There are advantages to being President.
The day after I was elected, I had my high school
grades classified Top Secret.

—RONALD REAGAN

"

Frankly, I don't mind not being President.
I just mind that someone else is.

—EDWARD KENNEDY

"

My early choice in life was either to be a piano
player in a whorehouse or a politician. And to tell the
truth, there's hardly any difference.

—HARRY TRUMAN

"

Being President is a lot like running
a cemetery. You've got a lot of people under
you and nobody's listening.

—BILL CLINTON

"

To those of you who received honours, awards and
distinctions, I say well done. And to the C students,
I say you, too, can be president of the United States.

—GEORGE W. BUSH

Being president is like being a jackass in a hailstorm.
There's nothing to do but stand there and take it.

—LYNDON JOHNSON

"

When the President does it,
that means that it's not illegal.

—RICHARD NIXON

"

Any man who wants to be president is
either an egomaniac or crazy.

—DWIGHT D. EISENHOWER

"

There are blessed intervals when I forget
by one means or another that I am
President of the United States.

—WOODROW WILSON

🐦 QUOTABLE TWEETS

I don't get the fuss about President's Day.
I spend my whole life not living up to promises
and nobody's giving me a holiday.

@HomerJSimpson

> "I am simple, complex, generous, selfish, unattractive, beautiful, lazy, and driven."
>
> —BARBARA STREISAND

AGE & BEAUTY

The older we get, the more we learn about the world—
or so we hope. It may not be fun to watch our faces and bodies
change over the years, but the life lessons we've learned are
reflected back at us each time we look in the mirror.

Love the One You've Got

Be happy in your body. . . . It's the only one
you've got, so you might as well like it.

—KEIRA KNIGHTLEY

"

I really don't think I need buns of steel.
I'd be happy with buns of cinnamon.

—ELLEN DEGENERES

I'm not overweight. I'm just nine inches too short.

—SHELLEY WINTERS

"

If you want to look young and thin,
hang around old fat people.

—JIM EASON

"

I'd rather be a few pounds heavier and enjoy
life than be worried all the time.

—DREW BARRYMORE

"

Even the worst haircut eventually grows out.

—LISA KOGAN

"

Happiness is the best facelift.

—DIANA KRALL

Beauty, to me, is about being comfortable in your
own skin. That, or a kick-ass red lipstick.
—GWYNETH PALTROW

"

I would rather be called funny than pretty.
—NIA VARDALOS

"

The most beautiful makeup for a woman is passion.
But cosmetics are easier to buy.
—YVES ST. LAURENT

"

It seems with every match I win,
I get better-looking to other people.
—ANDY RODDICK

"

It's great to be a blonde. With low expectations
it's very easy to surprise people.
—PAMELA ANDERSON

🐦 QUOTABLE TWEETS

It's all about lovin' not only who we see in the mirror, but
what we feel about ourselves when we look in the mirror.

@tyrabanks

Working It Out

I don't exercise. If God had wanted me to bend over,
he would have put diamonds on the floor.

—JOAN RIVERS

❝

The word aerobics came about when the gym instructors
got together and said, "If we're going to charge $10
an hour, we can't call it jumping up and down."

—RITA RUDNER

❝

I'm so unfamiliar with the gym I call it James.

—CHI MCBRIDE

"It's all right letting yourself
go, as long as you can get
yourself back."

—MICK JAGGER

To Your Health

The first wealth is health.

—RALPH WALDO EMERSON

"

The best beauty secret is sunblock.

—CHRISTIE BRINKLEY

"

Eat right, exercise regularly, die anyway.

—UNKNOWN

"

God gave us the gift of life; it is up to us
to give ourselves the gift of living well.

—VOLTAIRE

"

I believe that how you feel is very important to
how you look—that healthy equals beautiful.

—VICTORIA PRINCIPAL

I want to get old gracefully. I want to have
good posture, I want to be healthy and
be an example to my children.

—STING

"

Health nuts are going to feel stupid someday,
lying in hospitals dying of nothing.

—REDD FOXX

Making the Most of It

Life is too short to eat vanilla ice cream
and dance with boring men.

—UNKNOWN

"

You don't get to choose how you're going
to die. Or when. You can only decide
how you're going to live. Now.

—JOAN BAEZ

"

A life of unremitting caution, without the
carefree—or even, occasionally, the careless—
may turn out to be half a life.

—ANNA QUINDLEN

I'm learning in my old age that the only thing you can do to keep your sanity is to stay in the moment.

—WILLEM DAFOE

"

If Joan of Arc could turn the tide of an entire war before her 18th birthday, you can get out of bed.

—E. JEAN CARROLL

"

A diplomat is a man who always remembers a woman's birthday but never remembers her age.

—ROBERT FROST

Aging Well

You can get old pretty young if you don't take care of yourself.

—YOGI BERRA

"

The ball doesn't know how old I am.

—MARTINA NAVRATILOVA

"

I don't want to get to the end of my life and find that I have lived just the length of it. I want to have lived the width of it as well.

—DIANE ACKERMAN

THE PERFECT WORDS FOR

Get-Well Cards

I wonder why you can always read a doctor's bill
and you can never read his prescription.

—FINLEY PETER DUNNE

"

If you're going through hell, keep going.

—WINSTON CHURCHILL

"

Sleep, riches, and health to be truly
enjoyed must be interrupted.

—JOHANN PAUL FRIEDRICH RICHTER

"

When you come to the end of your rope,
tie a knot and hang on.

—FRANKLIN D. ROOSEVELT

"

To array a man's will against his sickness
is the supreme art of medicine.

—HENRY WARD BEECHER

"

Sickness comes on horseback but departs on foot.

—DUTCH PROVERB

In a sick-room or a bed-room there
should never be shutters shut.
—FLORENCE NIGHTINGALE

"

The only way to keep your health is to eat what you
don't want, drink what you don't like, and do what
you'd rather not.
—MARK TWAIN

"

Health is like money—we never have a true
idea of its value until we lose it.
—JOSH BILLINGS

"

My own prescription for health
is less paperwork and more running
barefoot through the grass.
—LESLIE GRIMUTTER

"

Early to bed and early
to rise, makes a man
healthy, wealthy, and wise.
—BENJAMIN FRANKLIN

The only thing that has ever made me feel old is those few times where I allow myself to be predictable.

—CARLOS SANTANA

"

The heart ages last.

—SYLVESTER STALLONE

"

Maturity is a high price to pay for growing up.

—TOM STOPPARD

"

I don't feel old. I don't feel anything till noon. That's when it's time for my nap.

—BOB HOPE

"

One day I woke up and I was the oldest person in every room.

—BILL CLINTON

"

Life asks us to make measurable progress in reasonable time. That's why they make those fourth-grade chairs so small—so you won't fit in them at age 25.

—JIM ROHN

"

The older I get, the better I used to be.

—JOHN MCENROE

Forget aging. If you're six feet above ground,
it's a good day.

—FAITH HILL

"

My father gave me the best advice of my life. He said,
"Whatever you do, don't wake up at 65 years old and
think about what you should have done with your life."

—GEORGE CLOONEY

"

The problem with beauty is that it's like
being born rich and getting poorer.

—JOAN COLLINS

"

Whether you're a man or not comes from your heart,
not how much hair you have on your head.

—BRUCE WILLIS

Some people might say, "Who would want to be 90?"
And I say, Anyone who is 89.

—PHYLLIS DILLER

"

Inside every old person is a younger person
wondering "What the hell happened?"

—CORA HARVEY ARMSTRONG

Feeling Young

....

The most sophisticated people I know—
inside they are all children.

—JIM HENSON

"

Adults are always asking children what
they want to be when they grow up because
they're looking for ideas.

—PAULA POUNDSTONE

"

The key to successful aging is to pay
as little attention to it as possible.

—JUDITH REGAN

"If only I'd known that one day my differentness would be an asset, then my early life would have been much easier."

—BETTE MIDLER

"

I'm sixty years of age. That's 16 Celsius.

—GEORGE CARLIN

"

Youth would be an ideal state if
it came a little later in life.

—HERBERT ASQUITH

"

Another belief of mine: that everyone else my age
is an adult, whereas I am merely in disguise.

—MARGARET ATWOOD

"

Everybody, no matter how old you are,
is around 24, 25 in their heart.

—BRUCE WILLIS

"

How old would you be if you didn't
know how old you are?

—LEROY "SATCHEL" PAGE

I feel young, but my body doesn't agree.
—BRYANT GUMBEL

"

When people ask me how old I am, I tell them
I'm 39—with 25 years of experience.
—CHUCK NORRIS

"

The aging process has you firmly in its grasp
if you never get the urge to throw a snowball.
—DOUG LARSON

"

Youth is a wonderful thing.
What a crime to waste it on children.
—GEORGE BERNARD SHAW

"

I will never be an old man. To me, old age
is always 15 years older than I am.
—FRANCIS BACON

The Benefits of Age

An archaeologist is the best husband
a woman can have. The older she gets
the more interested he is in her.
—AGATHA CHRISTIE

Wisdom comes with age, but keep it to yourself.

—MARY ROACH

"

Good judgment comes from experience, and often experience comes from bad judgment.

—RITA MAE BROWN

"

When you're over the hill, that's when you pick up speed.

—QUINCY JONES

"

My mother always used to say, "The older you get, the better you get. Unless you're a banana."

—BETTY WHITE

Memory Lane

Everybody needs his memories. They keep the wolf of insignificance from the door.

—SAUL BELLOW

"

Memory is a complicated thing, a relative to truth but not its twin.

—BARBARA KINGSOLVER

THE PERFECT WORDS FOR
Birthday Cards

One of the best parts of growing older? You can flirt
all you like since you've become harmless.

—LIZ SMITH

"

How old would you be if you didn't
know how old you are?

—SATCHEL PAIGE

"

The more you praise and celebrate your life,
the more there is in life to celebrate.

—OPRAH

"

You are only young once, but you can stay
immature indefinitely.

—OGDEN NASH

"

Age is an issue of mind over matter.
If you don't mind, it doesn't matter.

—MARK TWAIN

"

There is still no cure for the common birthday.

—JOHN GLENN

Middle age is the awkward period when Father Time
starts catching up with Mother Nature.

—HAROLD COFFIN

"

The secret of staying young is to live honestly,
eat slowly, and lie about your age.

—LUCILLE BALL

"

Birthdays are good for you. Statistics show that
the people who have the most live the longest.

—LARRY LORENZONI

"

Those who love deeply never
grow old; they may die of old
age, but they die young.

—DOROTHY CANFIELD FISHER

"

You know you're getting old
when the candles cost
more than the cake.

—BOB HOPE

🐦 QUOTABLE TWEETS

They say memory is the first thing to go.
The second thing to go is memory.

@GeorgeTakei

Memory is often less about the truth
than about what we want it to be.

—DAVID HALBERSTAM

"

Anything that triggers good memories
can't be all bad.

—ADAM WEST

"

A person without regrets is a nincompoop.

—MIA FARROW

"

Happiness is nothing more than good health
and a bad memory.

—ALBERT SCHWEITZER

"

It's surprising how much of memory is built
around things unnoticed at the time.

—BARBARA KINGSOLVER

I've got "Sometimers." Sometimes I remember
and sometimes I forget.

—SPIKE LEE

The Time We Have

I never think of the future. It comes soon enough.

—ALBERT EINSTEIN

"

How you spend your time is more important
than how you spend your money. Money mistakes
can be corrected, but time is gone forever.

—DAVID B. NORRIS

"

Time is an illusion. Lunchtime doubly so.

—DOUGLAS ADAMS

"

Time neither subtracts nor divides, but adds
at such a pace it seems like multiplication.

—BOB TALBERT

"

Eternity is a terrible thought. I mean,
where's it going to end?

—TOM STOPPARD

The future ain't what it used to be.
—YOGI BERRA

"

Forever is a long time, but not as long
as it was yesterday.
—DENNIS H'ORGNIES

"

Time goes, you say? Ah, no! Alas, Time stays, we go.
—AUSTIN DOBSON

"

Yesterday is a canceled check; tomorrow is a
promissory note; today is ready cash—use it.
—KAY LYONS

"

For disappearing acts, it's hard to beat
what happens to the eight hours supposedly left
after eight of sleep and eight of work.
—DOUG LARSON

A Beautiful World

Everybody needs beauty as well as bread,
places to play in and pray in, where nature may
heal and give strength to body and soul.
—JOHN MUIR

Unexpected intrusions of beauty. That is what life is.

—SAUL BELLOW

"

The most beautiful thing in the world is,
of course, the world itself.

—WALLACE STEVENS

"

Creativity is allowing yourself to make mistakes.
Art is knowing which ones to keep.

—SCOTT ADAMS

"

If truth is beauty, how come no one has
their hair done in the library?

—LILY TOMLIN

"

Normal day, let me be aware of the treasure you are.

—MARY JEAN IRION

"

Love beauty; it is the shadow of God on the universe.

—GABRIELA MISTRAL

Some people, no matter how old they get,
never lose their beauty—they merely move
it from their faces into their hearts.

—MARTIN BUXBAUM

"

Though we travel the world over to find the beautiful,
we must carry it with us or we find it not.

—RALPH WALDO EMERSON

"

People have the strength to overcome their
bodies. Their beauty is in their minds.

—PETER GABRIEL

"

Fashion is something that goes in one
year and out the other.

—DENISE KLAHN

No One Is Perfect

Your imperfections are what make you beautiful.

—SANDRA BULLOCK

"

Natural beauty takes at least two hours
in front of a mirror.

—PAMELA ANDERSON

Part of what makes a human being a human being is the imperfections. Like, you wouldn't give a robot my ears. You just wouldn't do that.

—WILL SMITH

"

It's not a bad thing, is it, to be strong in some ways and fragile and vulnerable in others?

—JENNIFER GARNER

"

It would be interesting to find out what goes on in that moment when someone looks at you and draws all sorts of conclusions.

—MALCOLM GLADWELL

"Summer is a drag because even normal people become obsessed with their bodies. A bad bathing suit can humiliate you more than anything else in life."

—CONAN O'BRIEN

THE PERFECT WORDS FOR

Retirement Speeches

The key to retirement is to find joy in the little things.

—SUSAN MILLER

"

People ask how I feel about getting old. I tell them
I have the same question. I'm learning as I go.

—PAUL SIMON

"

I'm not just retiring from the company,
I'm also retiring from my stress, my
commute, my alarm clock, and my iron.

—HARTMAN JULE

"

Retire? I can't spell the word.
I'd play in a wheelchair.

—KEITH RICHARDS

"

Life begins at retirement.

—UNKNOWN

"

There's one thing I always wanted
to do before I quit—retire!

—GROUCHO MARX

Retirement means no pressure, no stress,
no heartache . . . unless you play golf.

—GENE PERRET

"

It is time I stepped aside for a less experienced
and less able man.

—SCOTT ELLEDGE

"

The trouble with retirement is
that you never get a day off.

—ABE LEMONS

"

Retirement, a time to enjoy life! A time
to do what you want to do, when you want
to do it, how you want to do it.

—CATHERINE PULSIFER

"

When a man retires and time is no longer
a matter of urgent importance, his colleagues
generally present him with a watch.

—RC SHERIFF

"

Don't simply retire from something;
have something to retire to.

—HARRY EMERSON FOSDICK

> "Love is the answer, but while you're waiting for the answer, sex raises some pretty good questions."
>
> —WOODY ALLEN

LOVE & MARRIAGE

We can't live without love, but often living with it isn't that easy either. Gaining insight from different perspectives helps us understand our own relationships and be thankful for the one we've got.

Men on Marriage

Being a good husband is like being a stand-up comic. You need 10 years before you can even call yourself a beginner.

—JERRY SEINFELD

As a man in a relationship, you have a simple choice: You can be right or you can be happy.

—RALPHIE MAY

They say marriages are made in heaven. But so is thunder and lightning.

—CLINT EASTWOOD

If the marriage needs help, the answer almost always is have more fun. Drop your list of grievances and go ride a roller coaster.

—GARRISON KEILLOR

🐦 QUOTABLE TWEETS

No one in America should ever be afraid to walk down the street holding hands with the person they love.

@BarackObama

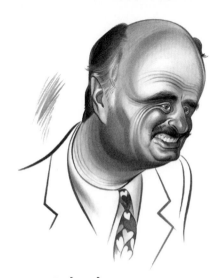

"If you marry for money you will earn every penny."

—DR. PHIL MCGRAW

Behind every great man is a woman rolling her eyes.

—JIM CARREY

I love being married. I was single for a long time, and I just got so sick of finishing my own sentences.

—BRIAN KILEY

My wife tells me that if I ever decide to leave, she's coming with me.

—JON BON JOVI

Never marry anyone you could not sit next to during a three-day bus trip.

—ROGER EBERT

Rituals are important. Nowadays it's hip not to be married. I'm not interested in being hip.

—JOHN LENNON

"

Here's the secret to a happy marriage:
Do what your wife tells you.

—DENZEL WASHINGTON

"

If you have a boat and a happy marriage,
you don't need another thing.

—ED MCMAHON

"

My parents just had their 50th anniversary and
they're happier than ever. They have each
other's back—I think that's what it's about.

—BEN STILLER

"

A happy home is one in which each spouse grants
the possibility that the other may be right,
though neither believes it.

—DON FRASER

"

My advice to you is get married: if you find a good wife
you'll be happy; if not, you'll become a philosopher.

—SOCRATES

No matter what kind of backgrounds
two men are from, if you go, "Hey, man, women
are crazy," you've got a friend.

—CHRIS ROCK

"

Almost no one is foolish enough to imagine that
he automatically deserves great success in any field
of activity; yet almost everyone believes that he
automatically deserves success in marriage.

—SYDNEY J. HARRIS

Women on Marriage

Sexiness wears thin after a while, and beauty fades,
but to be married to a man who makes you laugh
every day, ah, now that's a real treat.

—JOANNE WOODWARD

🐦 QUOTABLE TWEETS

Don't make mountains out of molehills. If your partner
says that everything is OK, believe it.

@AskDrRuth

At every party, there are two kinds of people—
those who want to go home and those who don't.
The trouble is, they are usually married to each other.

—ANN LANDERS

"

Grief is the price we pay for love.

—QUEEN ELIZABETH II

"

Marriage is very difficult. It's like a 5,000-piece
jigsaw puzzle, all sky.

—CATHY LADMAN

"

The opposite of love isn't hate—it's indifference.
And if you hate me, that means you still care.

—MARCIA CROSS

"

It is only when you see people looking ridiculous
that you realize just how much you love them.

—AGATHA CHRISTIE

"

The three words every woman really
longs to hear: I'll clean up.

—MOLLY SHANNON

"

Love is blind, but marriage is a real eye-opener.

—PAULA DEEN

One of the few articles of clothing that a man
won't try to remove from a woman is an apron.

—MARILYN VOS SAVANT

"

Why does a woman work ten years to change
a man's habits and then complain that
he's not the man she married?

—BARBRA STREISAND

"

For marriage to be a success, every woman and every
man should have her and his own bathroom. The end.

—CATHERINE ZETA-JONES

"

Most of my life, if a man did something totally other
than the way I thought it should be done, I would try
to correct him. Now I say, "Oh, isn't that interesting?"

—ELLEN BURSTYN

"

I really do believe if you can live through remodeling
a home, you can live the rest of your lives together.

—JENNIFER ANISTON

"

In the early years, you fight because
you don't understand each other. In later
years, you fight because you do.

—JOAN DIDION

THE PERFECT WORDS FOR
Wedding Speeches

The formula for a successful relationship is simple:
Treat all disasters as if they were trivialities,
but never treat a triviality as if it were a disaster.
—QUENTIN CRISP

"

Marriage should, I think, always be a little hard
and new and strange. It should be breaking your shell
and going into another world, and a bigger one.
—ANNE MORROW LINDBERGH

"

Getting married is an incredible act of hopefulness.
—ASHLEY JUDD

"

Story writers say that love is concerned only with
young people, and the excitement and glamour of
romance end at the altar. How blind they are. The best
romance is inside marriage; the finest love stories
come after the wedding, not before.
—IRVING STONE

"

Love is a game that two can play and both win.
—EVA GABOR

A journey is like marriage. The certain way
to be wrong is to think you control it.

—JOHN STEINBECK

❝

Love doesn't just sit there, like a stone; it has to be
made, like bread, remade all the time, made new.

—URSULA K. LEGUIN

❝

Let there be spaces in your togetherness / And
let the winds of the heavens dance between you.

—KAHLIL GIBRAN

❝

In marriage, being the right person is as
important as finding the right person.

—WILBERT DONALD GOUGH

❝

The key to a long and healthy
marriage is that, honestly, there's
nothing worth fighting about.

—JAY LENO

❝

Marrying for love may be a bit risky, but it is
so honest that God can't help but smile on it.

—JOSH BILLINGS

We seldom give each other advice—I think
that's the success of 25 years of marriage.

—LAURA BUSH

"

Why leave the nut you got for one you don't know?

—LORETTA LYNN

Sex

Sex is good, but not as good as fresh sweet corn.

—GARRISON KEILLOR

"

If sex is such a natural phenomenon, how come
there are so many books on how to do it?

—BETTE MIDLER

"

Lust is what makes you keep wanting to do it, even
when you have no desire to be with each other. Love
is what makes you keep wanting to be with each
other, even when you have no desire to do it.

—JUDITH VIORST

A Little Heart

Want to improve your relationships?
See love as a verb rather than as a feeling.

—STEPHEN R. COVEY

❝

I know love at first sight can work.
It happened to my parents.

—GEORGE CLOONEY

❝

You know how they say we only use 10 percent of our brains? I think we only use 10 percent of our hearts.

—OWEN WILSON

❝

In a nutshell, loving someone is about giving, not receiving.

—NICHOLAS SPARKS

"To wear your heart on your sleeve isn't a very good plan. You should wear it inside, where it functions best."

—MARGARET THATCHER

I still believe that love is all you need. I don't know a better message than that.

—PAUL MCCARTNEY

"

If grass can grow through cement, love can find you at every time in your life.

—CHER

"

Love is like quicksilver in the hand. Leave the fingers open, and it stays. Clutch it, and it darts away.

—DOROTHY PARKER

Love is the net where hearts are caught like fish.

—MUHAMMAD ALI

"

Manners are love in a cool climate.

—QUENTIN CRISP

"

All our loves are first loves.

—SUSAN FROMBERG

"

What the world really needs is more love
and less paper work.

—PEARL BAILEY

Men & Women

Men forget everything; women remember everything.
That's why men need instant replays in sports.

—RITA RUDNER

THE PERFECT WORDS FOR

Anniversary Toasts

For two people in a marriage to live together
day after day is unquestionably the one
miracle the Vatican has overlooked.

—BILL COSBY

"

A wedding anniversary is the celebration of love,
trust, partnership, tolerance and tenacity.
The order varies for any given year.

—PAUL SWEENEY

"

A long marriage is two people trying to dance
a duet and two solos at the same time.

—ANNE TAYLOR FLEMING

"

Love is what you've been through with somebody.

—JAMES THURBER

"

A good marriage is like an incredible retirement
fund. You put everything you have into it
during your productive life, and over the years
it turns from silver to gold to platinum.

—WILLARD SCOTT

Love endures only when the lovers love many things together and not merely each other.

—WALTER LIPPMANN

"

Getting married is easy. Staying married is more difficult. Staying happily married for a lifetime should rank among the fine arts.

—ROBERTA FLACK

"

One advantage of marriage is that when you fall out of love with him or he falls out of love with you, it keeps you together until you fall in again.

—JUDITH VIORST

"

A successful marriage requires falling in love many times, always with the same person.

—MIGNON MCLAUGHLIN

"

You don't marry one person; you marry three: the person you think they are, the person they are, and the person they are going to become as the result of being married to you.

—RICHARD NEEDHAM

Men fall in love with their eyes.
Women fall in love with their ears.

—DR. PHIL MCGRAW

"

A man has to be Joe McCarthy to be called ruthless.
All a woman has to do is put you on hold.

—MARLO THOMAS

"

Sometimes I wonder if men and women really
suit each other. Perhaps they should live next
door and just visit now and then.

—KATHARINE HEPBURN

"

A woman can say more in a sigh than
a man can say in a sermon.

—ARNOLD HAULTAIN

"

Men want the same thing from their underwear
that they want from women: a little bit of support,
and a little bit of freedom.

—JERRY SEINFELD

"

Nobody will ever win the battle of the sexes.
There's too much fraternizing with the enemy.

—HENRY KISSINGER

Dating

You've got to date a lot of Volkswagens
before you get to your Porsche.

—DEBBY ATKINSON

"

Being in therapy is great. I spend an hour just talking
about myself. It's kinda like being the guy on a date.

—CAROLINE RHEA

"

Falling in love and having a relationship
are two different things.

—KEANU REEVES

"

I don't have a girlfriend. But I do know a woman
who'd be mad at me for saying that.

—MITCH HEDBERG

QUOTABLE TWEETS

Women fall in love on the date, and
men fall in love after the date.

@pattistranger

Attraction

I like to have nice conversations with a man that teach me something, make me mad, make me curious. Then I find him attractive.

—RENEE ZELLWEGER

"

Obviously I have this strange animal magnetism. It's very hard to take my eyes off myself.

—MICK JAGGER

"

"I've reached the age where competence is a turn-on."

—BILLY JOEL

To my eye, women get sexier around 35. They know a thing or two, and knowledge is always alluring.

—PIERCE BROSNAN

The perfect man? A poet on a motorcycle.

—LUCINDA WILLIAMS

"

I like a woman with a head on her shoulders.
I hate necks.

—STEVE MARTIN

"

Honesty is probably the sexiest thing
a man can give to a woman.

—DEBRA MESSING

"

Flirting is conversational chemistry.

—ISAAC MIZRAHI

"

Sex appeal is fifty percent what you've got and
fifty percent what people think you've got.

—SOPHIA LOREN

What Is It Good For?

When you have no one in your life who you
can call and say, "I'm scared," then your life is
unfulfilling. You need somebody you can
trust enough to say, "I need help."

—STEVEN SODERBERGH

When love is your greatest weakness,
you will be the strongest person in the world.

—GARMAN WOLD

"

Passion makes the world go round.
Love just makes it a safer place.

—ICE-T

"

It's useless to hold a person to anything he says
when he's in love, drunk or running for office.

—SHIRLEY MACLAINE

Talk It Out

It is all right to hold a conversation,
but you should let go of it now and then.

—RICHARD ARMOUR

"

I have never been hurt by what I have not said.

—CALVIN COOLIDGE

"

I never learned anything while I was talking.

—LARRY KING

Having to explain it means you probably
shouldn't have said it.

—CARY CLACK

"

Real listening is a willingness to let
the other person change you.

—ALAN ALDA

"

When you don't know what you're talking about,
it's hard to know when you're finished.

—TOMMY SMOTHERS

"

Eighty percent of all questions are
statements in disguise.

—DR. PHIL MCGRAW

"

One thing I have learned is, if people tell you
they had a "frank" discussion with someone, it is
usually code for a yelling match with clenched fists.

—LARRY KING

"

When we criticize another person, it says nothing
about that person; it merely says something about
our own need to be critical.

—RICHARD CARLSON

THE PERFECT WORDS FOR

Love Letters

How in hell can you handle love without turning your life upside down? That's what love does, it changes everything.

—LAUREN BACALL

"

Love makes intellectual pretzels of us all.

—SARAH BIRD

"

Know that I love you and no matter what, I'll see you again.

—BRIAN SWEENEY

"

When the heart speaks, the mind finds it indecent to object.

—MILAN KUNDERA

"

In true love the smallest distance is too great, and the greatest distance can be bridged.

—HANS NOUWENS

"

In love, one and one are one

—JEAN-PAUL SARTRE

This is the true measure of love: when we believe
that we alone can love, that no one could
ever have loved so before us, and that no one
will ever love in the same way after us.
—JOHANN WOLFGANG VON GOETHE

"

I love you, not only for what you are,
but for what I am when I am with you.
—ROY CROFT

"

As soon go kindle fire with snow, as seek to
quench the fire of love with words.
—WILLIAM SHAKESPEARE

"

There are a lot of things
happening that show us that this,
right now, is a time to love.
—STEVIE WONDER

"

I was born when you kissed me.
I died when you left me. I lived a
few weeks while you loved me.
—HUMPHREY BOGART

Love Hurts

Love is a great wrecker of peace of mind.
—SUSAN CHEEVER

"

Jealousy is all the fun you think they had.
—ERICA JONG

"

You don't need to be a heroin addict
or a performance poet to experience extremity.
You just have to love someone.
—NICK HORNBY

"

Tests of love always end badly.
—MELANIE THERNSTROM

"

Women are like the police. They could have all the
evidence in the world, but they still want the confession.
—CHRIS ROCK

"

Assumptions are the termites of relationships.
—HENRY WINKLER

"

What are the three words guaranteed to humiliate
men everywhere? "Hold my purse."
—FRANÇOIS MORENCY

Love is never as ferocious as when you
think it's going to leave you.

—ANITA SHREVE

"

So many catastrophes in love are
only accidents of egotism.

—HECTOR BIANCIOTTI

"

Four be the things I'd have been better without:
love, curiosity, freckles and doubt.

—DOROTHY PARKER

"

Love is, or it ain't. Thin love ain't love at all.

—TONI MORRISON

"

It is often hard to bear the tears that
we ourselves have caused.

—MARCEL PROUST

> "Human beings are the only creatures on earth that allow their children to come back home."
>
> —BILL COSBY

FRIENDS & FAMILY

It has been said that family is everything: all there is, all your love, all your life. Families, and the friends that become as close as family, shape our worldview and inspire us to greatness.

Home Life

The ordinary acts we practice every day
at home are of more importance to the soul
than their simplicity might suggest.

—THOMAS MOORE

"

I still close my eyes and go home . . .
I can always draw from that.

—DOLLY PARTON

"

One's home is like a delicious piece of pie
you order in a restaurant on a country road one
cozy evening—the best piece of pie you have ever
eaten in your life—and can never find again.

—LEMONY SNICKET

"

Home is the place where, when you have
to go there, they have to take you in.

—ROBERT FROST

"

In most homes, the father is concerned with parking
space, the children with outer space, and the mother
with closet space.

—EVAN ESAR

The Meaning of Family

Acting is just a way of making a living;
the family is life.

—DENZEL WASHINGTON

No mater what you've done for yourself
or for humanity, if you can't look back on having
given love and attention to your own family,
what have you really accomplished?

—LEE IACOCCA

I'm not going to have a better day, a more magical
moment, than the first time I heard my daughter giggle.

—SEAN PENN

What is a family, after all, except memories?—
haphazard and precious as the contents
of a catchall drawer in the kitchen.

—JOYCE CAROL OATES

A family is a unit composed not only of
children but of men, women, an occasional
animal, and the common cold.

—OGDEN NASH

117

I would give everything if I could only keep my family.

—JOHNNY DEPP

"

You don't choose your family. They are God's
gift to you, as you are to them.

—DESMOND TUTU

"

Happiness is having a large, caring,
close-knit family in another city.

—GEORGE BURNS

"

Call it a clan, call it a network, call it a tribe, call it
a family. Whatever you call it, whoever you are, you
need one.

—JANE HOWARD

"

A happy family is but an earlier heaven.

—SIR JOHN BOWRING

🐦 QUOTABLE TWEETS

Your #family is depending on you. No better
reason to bring all your game all the time.

@GrantCardone

Children

Having children is like living in a frat house—
nobody sleeps, everything's broken and
there's a lot of throwing up.

—RAY ROMANO

66

I would be most content if my children grew up
to be the kind of people who think decorating consists
mostly of building enough bookshelves.

—ANNA QUINDLEN

66

Work is the least important thing
and family is the most important.

—JERRY SEINFELD

66

Ask your child what he wants for
dinner only if he's buying.

—FRAN LEBOWITZ

66

Everyone should have kids. They are the greatest
joy in the world. But they are also terrorists.
You'll realize this as soon as they are born and they
start using sleep deprivation to break you.

—RAY ROMANO

New-Baby Cards

I think, at a child's birth, if a mother could ask
a fairy godmother to endow it with the most useful
gift, that gift should be curiosity.

—ELEANOR ROOSEVELT

"

If you can give your child only one gift,
let it be enthusiasm.

—BRUCE BARTON

"

Making the decision to have a child is momentous.
It is to decide forever to have your heart go
walking around outside your body.

—ELIZABETH STONE

"

Having a baby is like falling in love again,
both with your husband and your child.

—TINA BROWN

"

Babies are bits of stardust, blown from
the hand of God. Lucky the woman who knows
the pangs of birth, for she has held a star.

—LARRY BARRATTO

Babies are such a nice way to start people.

—DON HEROLD

"

Every child begins the world again.

—HENRY DAVID THOREAU

"

Every baby born into the world is
a finer one than the last.

—CHARLES DICKENS

"

A baby is God's opinion that the world should go on.

—CARL SANDBURG

"

Having a child is surely the most beautifully irrational
act that two people in love can commit.

—BILL COSBY

"

A baby is born with a need to be loved—
and never outgrows it.

—FRANK A. CLARK

"

There are two things in this life for which
we are never fully prepared: twins.

—JOSH BILLINGSAD

The best way to keep children at home
is to make the home atmosphere pleasant—
and let the air out of the tires.
—DOROTHY PARKER

"

Having five children in six years is the best
training in the world for Speaker of the House.
—NANCY PELOSI

"

Just be good and kind to your children.
Not only are they the future of the world, they're
the ones who can sign you into the home.
—DENNIS MILLER

"Kids are life's only
guaranteed bona fide
upside surprise."

—JACK NICHOLSON

122

Children are paparazzi. They take your picture
when you don't want them to.
—JAMIE LEE CURTIS

"

Having a two-year-old is like having a blender
that you don't have the top for.
—JERRY SEINFELD

"

It's never too late for a happy childhood.
—GLORIA STEINEM

"

Kids. They're not easy. But there has
to be some penalty for sex.
—BILL MAHER

"

All of us have to recognize that we owe our children
more than we have been giving them.
—HILLARY CLINTON

🐦 QUOTABLE TWEETS

@ItsMyTyme09 biggest mistake in helping
underserved kids is NOT RAISING the BAR high
enough. Children will believe if you believe in them.

@Oprah

With kids, the days are long, but the years are short.

—JOHN LEGUIZAMO

❝

Raising kids makes most people, including me,
grow up at least a little.

—MADONNA

❝

As a child, the only clear thought
I had was "Get candy."

—JERRY SEINFELD

Parents

You can hit my father over the head with
a chair and he won't wake up, but my mother,
all you have to do to my mother is cough
somewhere in Siberia and she'll hear you.

—J. D. SALINGER

❝

A new survey found that 12 percent of parents
punish their kids by banning social-networking
sites. The other 88 percent punish their kids
by joining social-networking sites.

—JIMMY FALLON

Like all parents, my husband and I just do the best
we can, and hold our breath and hope we've set
aside enough money for our kids' therapy.

—MICHELLE PFEIFFER

"

Until you become a parent, you can't begin to discover
your capacity for strength, love and fatigue.

—PETER GALLAGHER

"

Imagine if you succeeded in making the world
perfect for your children what a shock the
rest of life would be for them.

—JOYCE MAYNARD

"

A rich person should leave his kids enough to
do something, but not enough to do nothing.

—WARREN BUFFETT

"

It is an act of love to say, "I believe in you
as my child, and you don't need my help."

—PETER BUFFETT

"

My parents treated me like I had a brain—
which, in turn, caused me to have one.

—DIANE LANE

125

A perfect parent is a person with excellent child-rearing theories and no actual children.

—DAVE BARRY

"

The only way we can ever teach a child to say "I'm sorry" is for him to hear it from our lips first.

—KEVIN LEMAN

"

Setting a good example for your children does nothing but increase their embarrassment.

—DOUG LARSON

On Mothers

The most remarkable thing about my mother is that for 30 years she served the family nothing but leftovers. The original meal has never been found.

—CALVIN TRILLIN

"

Mother is a verb, not a noun.

—SHONDA RHIMES

"

They say our mothers really know how to push our buttons—because they installed them.

—ROBIN WILLIAMS

The more I go through parenting, the more
I say I owe my mother an apology.

—RAY ROMANO

"

I know enough to know that when
you're in a pickle ... call Mom.

—JENNIFER GARNER

"

Motherhood is not for the fainthearted.
Frogs, skinned knees and the insults of teenage
girls are not meant for the wimpy.

—DANIELLE STEELE

"

Nowadays they say you need to get a special
chip to put in the TV so kids can't watch this and that.
In my day, we didn't need a chip. My mom
was the chip. End of story.

—RAY CHARLES

If pregnancy were a book, they would
cut the last two chapters.

—NORA EPHRON

"

No one else, ever, will think you're great
the way your mother does.

—MARY MATALIN

"

My perspective on my mother has changed
immensely. She was a lot taller when I was younger.

—HOWIE MANDEL

On Fathers

It doesn't matter who my father was;
it matters who I remember he was.

—ANNE SEXTON

"

What's a good investment? Go home from
work early and spend the afternoon throwing
a ball around with your son.

—BEN STEIN

"

You know what's cool? My kids think I'm ordinary.

—MICHAEL J. FOX

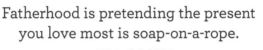

"I haven't taught people in
50 years what my father taught
by example in one week."

—MARIO CUOMO

Fatherhood is pretending the present
you love most is soap-on-a-rope.

—BILL COSBY

"

The most important thing a father can do
for his children is to love their mother.

—REV. THEODORE HESBURGH

"

The best thing I've ever done? Well, I've created four
beautiful children. You mean, other than that?

—DONALD TRUMP

"

Being a dad is the greatest, except for assembling things.

—CONAN O'BRIEN

THE PERFECT WORDS FOR

Cards for Mom

I remember my mother's prayers and they have always
followed me. They have clung to me all my life.

—ABRAHAM LINCOLN

"

The heart of a mother is a deep abyss at the bottom
of which you will always find forgiveness.

—HONORÉ DE BALZAC

"

Mother love is the fuel that enables a normal
human being to do the impossible.

—MARION C. GARRETTY

"

[A] mother is one to whom you hurry
when you are troubled.

—EMILY DICKINSON

"

A mother is the truest friend we have . . .

—WASHINGTON IRVING

"

There's nothing like a mama-hug.

—ADABELLA RADICI

When it comes to raising children, I believe in give and take. I give orders and they take 'em.

—BERNIE MAC

Parental Advice

My father used to say, "If you want to be different, do something different."

—WYNTON MARSALIS

"

My mom always said normal is just a cycle on the washing machine.

—WYNONNA JUDD

"

My father used to say, "Don't raise your voice. Improve your argument."

—DESMOND TUTU

When your mother asks, "Do you want a piece of advice?" it is a mere formality. It doesn't matter if you answer yes or no. You're going to get it anyway.

—ERMA BOMBECK

"

My father said there were two kinds of people in the world: givers and takers. The takers may eat better, but the givers sleep better.

—MARLO THOMAS

"

I have found the best way to give advice to your children is to find out what they want and then advise them to do it.

—HARRY TRUMAN

"

My dad once said, you wouldn't worry so much about what people thought of you if you knew how seldom they did.

—DR. PHIL MCGRAW

🐦 QUOTABLE TWEETS

I always dreamed about being a pro QB but more than anything, I wanted to be like my dad.

@TimTebow

If you want your kids to listen to you,
don't yell at them. Whisper. Make them lean in.
My kids taught me that. I do it with adults now.

—MARIO BATALI

Friends

....

A true friend is one who overlooks your failures
and tolerates your successes.

—DOUG LARSON

"

The true friend is the one that's coming in the door
while everyone else is going out.

—DR. PHIL MCGRAW

"

To remember friendship is to recall those conversations
that it seemed a sin to break off: the ones that made
the sacrifice of the following day a trivial one.

—CHRISTOPHER HITCHENS

"

You can always tell a real friend: when
you make a fool of yourself, he doesn't feel
you've done a permanent job.

—LAURENCE PETER

THE PERFECT WORDS FOR

Cards for Dad

A father carries pictures where his money used to be.
—UNKNOWN

"

Directly after God in heaven comes a Papa.
—MOZART

"

Blessed indeed is the man who hears
many gentle voices call him father!
—LYDIA CHILD

"

One father is more than a hundred schoolmasters.
—GEORGE HERBERT

"

By the time a man realizes that maybe his father was
right, he usually has a son who thinks he's wrong.
—CHARLES WADSWORTH

"

[My father] didn't tell me how to live;
he lived, and let me watch him do it.
—CLARENCE B. KELLAND

Friends are the family you choose.

—JENNIFER ANISTON

"

What is it about friendship that makes being among friends so much richer than being among the most accomplished and interesting strangers?

SANDY SHEEHY

"

One does not make friends. One recognizes them.

GARTH HENRICHS

"

Ask friends about the people and places that shaped them, and summer springs up quickly when they tell their story: their first kiss, first beer, first job that changed everything.

—NANCY GIBBS

"

You don't have to have anything in common with people you've known since you were five. With old friends, you've got your whole life in common.

—LYLE LOVETT

"

The only way to have a friend is to be one.

—RALPH WALDO EMERSON

The bird a nest, the spider a web, man friendship.

—WILLIAM BLAKE

"

Strangers are friends that you have yet to meet.

—ROBERTA LIEBERMAN

"

Be slow in choosing a friend, slower in changing.

—BENJAMIN FRANKLIN

"

The most called-upon prerequisite of a friend
is an accessible ear.

—MAYA ANGELOU

"

Some of the most rewarding and beautiful
moments of a friendship happen in the unforeseen
open spaces between planned activities. It is
important that you allow these spaces to exist.

—CHRISTINE LEEFELDT AND ERNEST CALLENBACH

"

A friend is someone who can see through
you and still enjoys the show.

—FARMERS' ALMANAC

"

Friends are those rare people who ask how
we are and then wait to hear the answer.

—ED CUNNINGHAM

We love those who know the worst of us
and don't turn their faces away.

—WALKER PERCY

"

No man can be called friendless when he has
God and the companionship of good books.

—ELIZABETH BARRETT BROWNING

What Friends Are For

I value the friend who for me finds time
on his calendar, but I cherish the friend who
for me does not consult his calendar.

—ROBERT BRAULT

"

Don't make friends who are comfortable to be with.
Make friends who will force you to lever yourself up.

—THOMAS J. WATSON SR.

🐦 QUOTABLE TWEETS

A true #friend is someone who thinks that you are a good
egg even though he knows you are slightly cracked.

@Chr1stlike (Rigo Campos)

"The proper office of
a friend is to side
with you when you
are in the wrong.
Nearly anybody will
side with you when
you are right."

—MARK TWAIN

Lots of people want to ride with you in the limo,
but what you want is someone who will take the
bus with you when the limo breaks down.

—OPRAH

"

A loyal friend laughs at your jokes when
they're not so good, and sympathizes with
your problems when they're not so bad.

—ARNOLD H. GLASOW

"

We need old friends to help us grow old
and new friends to help us stay young.

—LETTY COTTIN POGREBIN

138

If you want an accounting of your worth,
count your friends.

—MERRY BROWNE

"

We cherish our friends not for their ability to amuse
us, but for our ability to amuse them.

—EVELYN WAUGH

"

A true friend never gets in your way unless you
happen to be going down.

—ARNOLD H. GLASOW

"

Only your real friends will tell you when your face is dirty.

—SICILIAN PROVERB

"

A friend is someone who makes you
feel totally acceptable.

—ENE RIISNA

🐦 QUOTABLE TWEETS

putting our expectations on others is an exercise
in #pressure &disappointment. why not accept
people just as they are? that's #love xoP

@PaulaAbdul

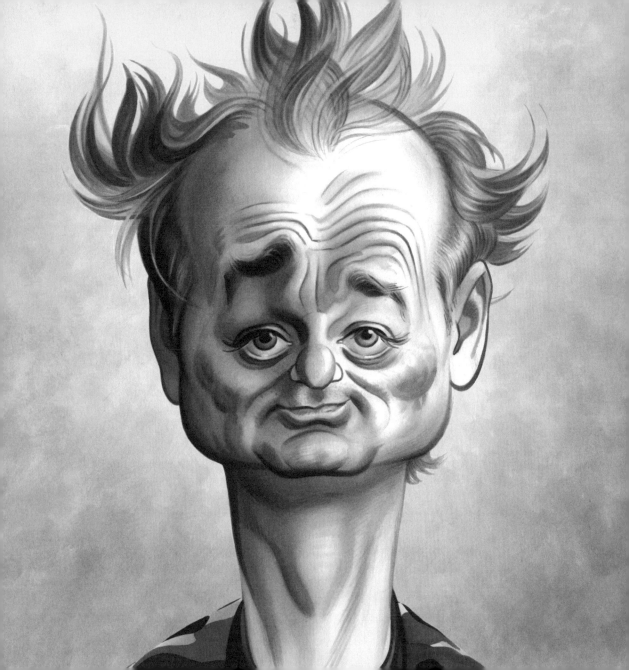

"There's only now."

—BILL MURRAY

THE GOOD LIFE

Hard work pays off in the moments that are filled with beauty—the ones that allow us to sit back, take a deep breath, and elate in that which we truly enjoy.

Kicking Back

There's never enough time to do all the nothing you want.

—BILL WATTERSON

"

For fast-acting relief, try slowing down.

—LILY TOMLIN

"

Sometimes the most important thing in a whole day
is the rest we take between two deep breaths.

—ETTY HILLESUM

"

Doing nothing is very hard to do—you never
know when you're finished.

—LESLIE NIELSEN

"

Bed is like the womb, only drier
and with better TV reception.

—LINDA RICHMAN

🐦 QUOTABLE TWEETS

Life is supposed to be fun! When you're having fun,
you feel great and you receive great things!

@ByrneRhonda

How many inner resources one needs to tolerate
a life of leisure without fatigue.

—NATALIE CLIFFORD BARNEY

Time you enjoy wasting was not wasted.

—JOHN LENNON

Food

There is no love sincerer than the love of food.

—GEORGE BERNARD SHAW

The only time to eat diet food is while
you're waiting for the steak to cook.

—JULIA CHILD

The trouble with eating Italian food is that
five or six days later, you're hungry again.

—GEORGE MILLER

Large, naked, raw carrots are acceptable as food only
to those who live in hutches eagerly awaiting Easter.

—FRAN LEBOWITZ

Never eat more than you can lift.

—MISS PIGGY

"

You cannot truly say you live well unless you eat well.

—NIGELLA LAWSON

"

It's okay to play with your food.

—EMERIL LAGASSE

"

Vegetables are a must on a diet. I suggest carrot cake, zucchini bread and pumpkin pie.

—JIM DAVIS

"One of the very nicest things about life is the way we must regularly stop whatever it is we are doing and devote our attention to eating."

—LUCIANO PAVAROTTI

A good slice of pizza can be as good
as a $200 meal in a restaurant.
—BENICIO DEL TORO

"

Life is too short to drink the house wine.
—HELEN THOMAS

"

Just try to be angry with someone
who fed you something delicious.
—CARMEN COOK

"

Stress cannot exist in the presence of a pie.
—DAVID MAMET

Travel & Vacations

Not all those who wander are lost.
—J. R. R. TOLKIEN

"

Travel is fatal to prejudice, bigotry,
and narrow-mindedness.
—MARK TWAIN

"

I'm still ready to go to the moon, if they'll take me.
—WALTER CRONKITE

THE PERFECT WORDS FOR
Invitations

Life is not dated merely by years.
Events are sometimes the best calendars.

—BENJAMIN DISRAELI

"

You only live once. But if you work
it right, once is enough.

—FRED ALLEN

"

We are all mortal until the first kiss and
the second glass of wine.

—EDUARDO GALEANO

"

Is not life a hundred times too short
for us to bore ourselves?

—FRIEDRICH NIETZSCHE

"

Dance till the stars come down from the rafters!
Dance, Dance, Dance till you drop!

—W. H. AUDEN

Karaoke is the great equalizer.

—AISHA TYLER

"

We're fools whether we dance or not,
so we might as well dance.

—JAPANESE PROVERB

"

When wine goes in strange things come out.

—FRIEDRICH SCHILLER

"

Drink, and dance and laugh and lie,
Love the reeling midnight through,
For tomorrow we shall die!
(But, alas, we never do.)

—DOROTHY PARKER

"

Spend the afternoon. You can't take it with you.

—ANNIE DILLARD

"

There is no cure for birth and death,
save to enjoy the interval.

—GEORGE SANTAYANA

🐦 QUOTABLE TWEETS

You knows what's amazing about life.
Enjoying what you see.

@dennisrodman

Airplane travel is nature's way of making
you look like your passport photo.

—AL GORE

"

Most of American life is driving somewhere and then
driving back wondering why the hell you went.

—JOHN UPDIKE

"

If you don't know where you're going,
any road will take you there.

—GEORGE HARRISON

"

Travel is glamorous only in retrospect.

—PAUL THEROUX

"

Camping: nature's way of promoting the motel industry.

—DAVE BARRY

Holidays

No matter how carefully you stored the lights last year, they will be snarled again this Christmas.

—ROBERT KIRBY

"

Christmas: It's the only religious holiday that's also a federal holiday. That way, Christians can go to their services, and everyone else can sit at home and reflect on the true meaning of the separation of church and state.

—SAMANTHA BEE

"

I get really grinchy right up until Christmas morning.

—DAN AYKROYD

"

Christmas is a time when everybody wants his past forgotten and his present remembered.

—PHYLLIS DILLER

"

Oh, joy, Christmas Eve. By this time tomorrow, millions of Americans, knee-deep in tinsel and wrapping paper, will utter those heartfelt words: "Is this all I got?"

—KELSEY GRAMMER

Oh, volunteer work! That's what I like about the holiday season. That's the true spirit of Christmas. People being helped by people other than me.

—JERRY SEINFELD

"

We're having something a little different this year for Thanksgiving. Instead of a turkey, we're having a swan. You get more stuffing.

—GEORGE CARLIN

"

Thanksgiving is the one occasion each year when gluttony becomes a patriotic duty.

—MICHAEL DRESSER

"Airport screeners are now scanning holiday fruitcakes. Not even the scanners can tell what those little red things are."

—DAVID LETTERMAN

The Road to Happiness

The most likely moment for something incredible
to happen to me was the moment I was most
certain nothing ever would.

—JANE PAULEY

"

The firsts go away—first love, first baby,
first kiss. You have to create new ones.

—SARAH JESSICA PARKER

"

Sometimes when almost everything is wrong,
one thing is so right you would do it all again.

—ALICE RANDALL

"

Let's face it, all the good stuff happens after midnight.

—MATT GROENING

"

Don't waste a minute not being happy. If one window
closes, run to the next window—or break down a door.

—BROOKE SHIELDS

"

I have enjoyed life a lot more by
saying yes than by saying no.

—RICHARD BRANSON

> "Joy is one of the only emotions you can't contrive."
>
> —BONO

There are some things in life where it's better to receive than to give, and massage is one of them.

—AL MICHAELS

"

A happy heart comes first, then the happy face.

—SHANIA TWAIN

"

I might not be famous one day. But I'd still be happy.

—SALMA HAYEK

"

The only way to have a life is to commit to it like crazy.

—ANGELINA JOLIE

> Good morning/afternoon/evening/night. Wherever you are in your day, I hope you're laughing.
>
> @Alyssa_Milano

Happiness hides in life's small details.
If you're not looking, it becomes invisible.
—JOYCE BROTHERS

Books & Stories

Always read the stuff that will make you look
good if you die in the middle of it.
—P. J. O'ROURKE

If there's a book you really want to read, but it
hasn't been written yet, then you must write it.
—TONI MORRISON

The mark of a good book is it changes
every time you read it.
—ANDERSON COOPER

THE PERFECT WORDS FOR
Holiday Cards

A lovely thing about Christmas is that it's compulsory, like a thunderstorm, and we all go through it together.

—GARRISON KEILLOR

"

The darkness of the whole world cannot swallow the glowing of a candle.

—ROBERT ALTINGER

"

At Christmas play and make good cheer, for Christmas comes but once a year.

—THOMAS TUSSER

"

Christmas gift suggestions: to your enemy, forgiveness. To an opponent, tolerance. To a friend, your heart. To a customer, service. To all, charity. To every child, a good example. To yourself, respect.

—OREN ARNOLD

"

Christmas is not a time or a season but a state of mind. To cherish peace and good will, to be plenteous in mercy, is to have the real spirit of Christmas.

—CALVIN COOLIDGE

The best of all gifts around any Christmas tree: the presence of a happy family all wrapped up in each other.

—BURTON HILLIS

"

New Year's is every man's birthday.

—CHARLES LAMB

"

Christmas waves a magic wand over this world, and behold, everything is softer and more beautiful.

—NORMAN VINCENT PEALE

"

Cheers to a new year and another chance for us to get it right.

—OPRAH

"

One of the most glorious messes in the world is the mess created in the living room on Christmas Day. Don't clean it up too quickly.

—ANDY ROONEY

"

May Peace be your gift at Christmas and your blessing all year through!

—UNKNOWN

🐦 QUOTABLE TWEETS

@x_elenatheresa Books should always be open.
@CormacMcCarthys

Reading gives us someplace to go when
we have to stay where we are.
—MASON COOLEY

"

The first lesson reading teaches is how to be alone.
—JONATHAN FRANZEN

"

A good book is like an unreachable itch.
You just can't leave it alone.
—LAURA BUSH

"

I've written 17 novels, and I've found out that
fiction can't keep up with real life.
—JOHN GRISHAM

"

Don't judge a book by its cover 'til you've read the book.
—JAMIE LEE CURTIS

God made man because he loves stories.
—ELIE WIESEL

The most important part of a story is the ending.
No one reads a book to get to the middle.
—MICKEY SPILLANE

The dark night was the first book of poetry,
and the constellations were the poems.
—CHET RAYMO

A good story is at its best when the line between
truth and fiction remains ambiguous.
—LEICESTER HEMINGWAY

"You can't write poetry
on the computer."
—QUENTIN TARANTINO

Music

Country music has always been the best
shrink that 15 bucks can buy.

—DIERKS BENTLEY

"

Where words fail, music speaks.

—HANS CHRISTIAN ANDERSON

"

Every musical phrase has a purpose. It's like talking.
If you talk with a particular purpose, people listen to
you, but if you just recite, it's not as meaningful.

—ITZHAK PERLMAN

"

Great music is as much about the space between
the notes as it is about the notes themselves.

—STING

"

I think my music is like anchovies—some
people like it, some people get nauseous.

—BARRY MANILOW

"

Talking about music is like talking about sex.
Can you describe it? Are you supposed to?

—BRUCE SPRINGSTEEN

@WesleyStace Well try to finish before the show. The best music is recorded before 7pm, so your muse can replenish itself drinking at night.

@EugeneMirman

Jazz is democracy in music.

—WYNTON MARSALIS

"

What in the world would I sing for if I had it all?

—DAVE MATTHEWS

"

Rock is so much fun. That's what it's all about—filling up the chest cavities and empty kneecaps and elbows.

—JIMI HENDRIX

"

Music is the shorthand of emotion.

—LEO TOLSTOY

"

Without music, life is a journey through a desert.

—PAT CONROY

"

Music is a higher revelation than philosophy.

—LUDWIG VAN BEETHOVEN

Art

The practice of art isn't to make a living.
It's to make your soul grow.

—KURT VONNEGUT

"

Art is so wonderfully irrational, exuberantly
pointless, but necessary all the same.

—GÜNTER GRASS

"

I feel strongly that the visual arts are of vast importance.
Of course I could be prejudiced. I am a visual art.

—KERMIT THE FROG

"

All great art comes from a sense of outrage.

—GLENN CLOSE

"

Art doesn't reproduce the visible but
rather makes it visible.

—PAUL KLEE

"

Art extends each man's short time on earth
by carrying from man to man the whole
complexity of other men's lifelong experience,
with all its burdens, colors and flavor.

—ALEKSANDR SOLZHENITSYN

160

Art is a staple, like bread or wine or a warm coat in winter. Man's spirit grows hungry for art in the same way his stomach growls for food.

—IRVING STONE

"

Art is the signature of civilization.

—BEVERLY SILLS

"

What is freedom of expression? Without the freedom to offend, it ceases to exist.

—SALMAN RUSHDIE

"

Anyone who says you can't see a thought simply doesn't know art.

—WYNETKA ANN REYNOLDS

"

Art is the only way to run away without leaving home.

—TWYLA THARP

"

No great artist ever sees things as they really are. If he did, he would cease to be an artist.

—OSCAR WILDE

"

Art is the demonstration that the ordinary is extraordinary.

—AMÉDÉE OZENFANT

Quotable Movies

Love means never having to say you're sorry.
—*LOVE STORY*

"

Frankly, my dear, I don't give a damn.
—*GONE WITH THE WIND*

"

Nobody puts Baby in the corner.
—*DIRTY DANCING*

"

Carpe diem. Seize the day, boys.
Make your lives extraordinary.
—*DEAD POETS SOCIETY*

"

Gentlemen, you can't fight in here!
This is the War Room!
—*DR. STRANGELOVE*

"

Mama always said life was like a box of
chocolates. You never know what you're gonna get.
—*FORREST GUMP*

You're gonna need a bigger boat.

—*JAWS*

"

Toto, I've got a feeling we're not in Kansas anymore.

—*THE WIZARD OF OZ*

"

I love the smell of napalm in the morning.

—*APOCALYPSE NOW*

"

We must all face the choice between
what is right and what is easy.

—*HARRY POTTER AND THE GOBLET OF FIRE*

"

It doesn't take much to see that the problems
of three little people don't amount to a hill
of beans in this crazy world.

—*CASABLANCA*

"

I fart in your general direction. Your mother was
a hamster and your father smelt of elderberries.

—*MONTY PYTHON AND THE HOLY GRAIL*

"

Leave the gun, take the cannoli.

—*THE GODFATHER*

Sports

Everything at a baseball game is a little brighter,
a little sharper, a little more in focus. It's a magical
break from the worries and cares of everyday life.

—LARRY KING

"

If I'm winning, I have to act like I'm not bored.
If it's a tough match, I act like I'm having a
good time. I'm a drama queen.

—SERENA WILLIAMS

"

There's more to boxing than hitting.
There's not getting hit, for instance.

—GEORGE FOREMAN

"

Baseball, it is said, is only a game. True.
And the Grand Canyon is only a hole in Arizona.

—GEORGE WILL

🐦 QUOTABLE TWEETS

I'm starting to think that Jesus does love football.

@aplusk (Ashton Kutcher)

The moment of victory is much too short to live
for that and nothing else.
—MARTINA NAVRATILOVA

Technology

....

Man has made many machines, complex
and cunning, but which of them indeed rivals
the workings of his heart?
—PABLO CASALS

"

We live in a society exquisitely dependent on
science and technology, in which hardly anyone
knows anything about science and technology.
—CARL SAGAN

"

Any sufficiently advanced technology is
indistinguishable from magic.
—ARTHUR C. CLARKE

"

A computer once beat me at chess, but it was
no match for me at kickboxing.
—EMO PHILIPS

> "I like to crack the jokes now and again, but it's only because I struggle with math."
>
> —TINA FEY

LIFE IS HILARIOUS

Keeping a sense of humor about life, the universe, and everything is essential to keeping sane. Laughter is immediate relief for whatever ails you, and we're lucky that there are so many notable people practicing the therapeutic art of comedy.

Laughter, the Best Medicine

If there's one thing I know, it's that
God does love a good joke.

—HUGH ELLIOTT

"

Laughter brings the swelling down
on our national psyche.

—STEPHEN COLBERT

"

I am thankful for laughter, except when
milk comes out my nose.

—WOODY ALLEN

"

Nothing to me feels as good as
laughing incredibly hard.

—STEVE CARELL

"

I wake up laughing every day. I get a kick out of life.

—BRUCE WILLIS

"

Laughter is the shortest distance between two people.

—VICTOR BORGE

Whoever established the high road, and how
high it should be, should be fired.

—SANDRA BULLOCK

Tell me what you laugh at, and I'll tell you who you are.

—MARCEL PAGNOL

Laughter is an instant vacation.

—MILTON BERLE

You can't deny laughter. When it comes, it plops down
in your favorite chair and stays as long as it wants.

—STEPHEN KING

Comedy is like catching lightning in a bottle.

—GOLDIE HAWN

I'm not funny. What I am is brave.

—LUCILLE BALL

The only way you can know where
the line is, is if you cross it.

—DAVE CHAPPELLE

Good taste is the enemy of comedy.

—MEL BROOKS

169

Humor is a rubber sword—it allows you to make
a point without drawing blood.

—MARY HIRSCH

"

I'd rather be funny than wise.

—DENNIS MILLER

"

The highlight of my childhood was making my brother
laugh so hard that food came out of his nose.

—GARRISON KEILLOR

"

Wit is the key, I think, to anybody's heart.
Show me the person who doesn't like to laugh and
I'll show you a person with a toe tag.

—JULIA ROBERTS

"

Laughter and tears are both responses to frustration
and exhaustion . . . I myself prefer to laugh, since there
is less cleaning up to do afterward.

—KURT VONNEGUT

"

You can't stay mad at somebody who makes you laugh.

—JAY LENO

Look at Bob Hope. Look at Milton Berle, George Burns.
Look how long they lived. Seeing the funny side
of things keeps you alive.

—PHYLLIS DILLER

"

Never be afraid to laugh at yourself. After all, you
could be missing out on the joke of the century.

—DAME EDNA EVERAGE

"

There is no such thing as an attention span. People
have infinite attention if you are entertaining them.

—JERRY SEINFELD

"

I couldn't tell a joke if my life depended on it.

—DIANE KEATON

"

One doesn't have a sense of humor. It has you.

—LARRY GELBART

THE PERFECT WORDS FOR

Roasts

His mother should have thrown him
away and kept the stork.

—MAE WEST

"

[He was] one of the nicest old ladies I ever met.

—WILLIAM FAULKNER

"

He may look like an idiot and talk like an idiot,
but don't let that fool you, he really is an idiot.

—GROUCHO MARX

"

I will always love the false image I had of you.

—ASHLEIGH BRILLIANT

"

A modest little person, with much to be modest about.

—WINSTON CHURCHILL

"

I've just learned about his illness.
Let's hope it's nothing trivial.

—IRVIN S. COBB

I do desire we may be better strangers.
—WILLIAM SHAKESPEARE

"

She tells enough white lies to ice a wedding cake.
—MARGOT ASQUITH

"

In order to avoid being called a flirt,
she always yielded easily.
—CHARLES, COUNT TALLEYRAND

"

He has no enemies, but is intensely disliked
by his friends.
—OSCAR WILDE

"

That woman speaks eighteen languages and
can't say no in any of them.
—DOROTHY PARKER

"

He loves nature in spite of what it did to him.
—FORREST TUCKER

"

There is nothing wrong with you that
reincarnation won't cure.
—JACK E. LEONARD

There's nothing better than a world where everybody's just trying to make each other laugh.

—MATTHEW PERRY

"

Humor is always based on a modicum of truth. Ever heard a joke about a father-in-law?

—DICK CLARK

"

Wrinkles only go where the smiles have been.

—JIMMY BUFFETT

Personally Speaking

I haven't the slightest idea how to change people, but still I keep a long list of prospective candidates just in case I should ever figure it out.

—DAVID SEDARIS

"

Great people talk about ideas, average people talk about things, and small people talk about wine.

—FRAN LEBOWITZ

"

The difference between Sly Stallone and me is that I am me and he is him.

—ARNOLD SCHWARZENEGGER

There's nothing like a gleam of humor to reassure you that a fellow human being is ticking inside a strange face.

—EVA HOFFMAN

"

A narcissist is someone better-looking than you are.

—GORE VIDAL

"

I'm better off not socializing. I make a better impression if I'm not around.

—CHRISTOPHER WALKEN

Life Lessons

A synonym is a word you use when you can't spell the first word you thought of.

—BURT BACHARACH

"

It's only when the tide goes out that you learn who's been swimming naked.

—WARREN BUFFETT

"

The difference between fiction and reality? Fiction has to make sense.

—TOM CLANCY

175

"There's no one way to dance. And that's kind of my philosophy about everything."

—ELLEN DEGENERES

The trouble with having an open mind, of course, is that people will insist on coming along and trying to put things in it.

—TERRY PRATCHETT

"

Men don't care what's on TV. They only care what else is on TV.

—JERRY SEINFELD

"

Without geography, you're nowhere.

—JIMMY BUFFETT

🐦 **QUOTABLE TWEETS**

Just taught my kids about taxes by eating
38% of their ice cream.

@ConanOBrien

God writes comedy but sometimes
has a slow audience.

—GARRISON KEILLOR

❝

The world can't end today, because it's
already tomorrow in Australia.

—CHARLES M. SCHULZ

❝

You have to remember one thing about
the will of the people: It wasn't that long ago
that we were swept away by the macarena.

—JON STEWART

❝

In real life, I assure you, there
is no such thing as algebra.

—FRAN LEBOWITZ

Ain't Love Grand?

Love is a snowmobile racing across the tundra and then suddenly it flips over, pinning you underneath. At night, the ice weasels come.

—MATT GROENING

"

Put your hand on a hot stove for a minute, and it seems like an hour. Sit with a pretty girl for an hour, and it seems like a minute. That's relativity.

—ALBERT EINSTEIN

"

I was married by a judge. I should have asked for a jury.

—GROUCHO MARX

"

A girl phoned me the other day and said, "Come on over. There's nobody home." I went over. Nobody was home.

—RODNEY DANGERFIELD

🐦 QUOTABLE TWEETS

I got laid at IKEA this morning. Assembling the woman took a while though.

@JudahWorldChamp (Judah Friedlander)

No man is truly married until he understands
every word his wife is NOT saying.

—UNKNOWN

"

The cable TV sex channels don't expand
our horizons, don't make us better people, and
don't come in clearly enough.

—BILL MAHER

Technology

If it keeps up, man will atrophy all his limbs
but the push-button finger.

—FRANK LLOYD WRIGHT

"

Because Google is so popular, it's conceited.
Have you tried misspelling something lately? See the
tone that it takes? "Um, did you mean . . . ?"

—ARJ BARKER

"

When I first heard about the campaign to get me
to host Saturday Night Live, I didn't know what
Facebook was. And now that I do know what it is,
I have to say, it sounds like a huge waste of time!

—BETTY WHITE

Laughter, the Best Advice

Don't take life too seriously, you'll
never get out of it alive.
—ELBERT HUBBARD

❝

Never miss a good chance to shut up.
—WILL ROGERS

❝

I always advise people never to give advice.
—P.G. WODEHOUSE

❝

Always and never are two words you should
always remember never to use.
—WENDELL JOHNSON

❝

Don't smoke too much, drink too much, eat too much
or work too much. We're all on the road to the grave—
but there's no need to be in the passing lane.
—ROBERT ORBEN

❝

I believe in an open mind, but not so open
that your brains fall out.
—ARTHUR HAYS SULZBERGER

A successful man is one who makes more money than his wife can spend. A successful woman is one who can find such a man.

—LANA TURNER

"

A word to the wise ain't necessary— it's the stupid ones that need the advice.

—BILL COSBY

"

If two wrongs don't make a right, try three.

—LAURENCE PETER

"

Don't worry about your heart. It will last as long as you live.

W.C. FIELDS

"

The next time you have a thought . . . let it go.

—RON WHITE

"

Any girl can be glamorous. All you have to do is stand still and look stupid.

—LAURENCE PETER

"Personally,
I'm waiting
for caller IQ."
—SANDRA BERNHARD

To err is human, but to really foul
things up you need a computer.
—PAUL EHRLICH

"

Computers make it easier to do a lot
of things, but most of the things they
make easier to do don't need to be done.
—ANDY ROONEY

"

I don't believe in e-mail. I'm an old-fashioned girl.
I prefer calling and hanging up.
—SARAH JESSICA PARKER

Why do I have to follow CNN on Twitter? If I want to follow CNN, I can follow them on CNN.

—JON STEWART

"

So I'm reading a book on my new iPad, but can't the iPad read it for me? Do I have to do everything?

—MATTHEW PERRY

"

E-mails are letters, after all, more lasting than phone calls, even if many of them r 2 cursory 4 u.

—ANNA QUINDLEN

Success!

Money frees you from doing things you dislike. Since I dislike doing nearly everything, money is handy.

—GROUCHO MARX

🐦 QUOTABLE TWEETS

Cleaning my hand print off of a mirror. Don't high-five your reflection. Just nod or wink.

@danecook

It's hard to do nothing because you tend to do something and then you have to drop everything.
—JERRY SEINFELD

"

The beaten path is the safest, but the traffic's terrible.
—JEFF TAYLOR

"

The safest way to double your money is to fold it over once and put it in your pocket.
—KIN HUBBARD

"

The only thing worse than beating a dead horse is betting on one.
—RELIENT K

"

You can't get spoiled if you do your own ironing.
—MERYL STREEP

"

They say you only go around once, but with a muscle car you can go around two or three times.
—TIM ALLEN

"

I am old enough to know that a red carpet is just a rug.
—AL GORE

Conversationally Speaking

Most people hate cell phone use on trains;
I love cell phone use on trains. What do you
want to do, read that report on your lap, or hear
about your neighbor's worst date ever?

—LIZA MUNDY

❝

The opposite of talking isn't listening.
The opposite of talking is waiting.

—FRAN LEBOWITZ

❝

I personally think we developed language because
of our deep inner need to complain.

—JANE WAGNER

185

People will accept your ideas much more readily
if you tell them Benjamin Franklin said it first.

—DAVID H. COMINS

"

Gossip is just news running ahead
of itself in a red satin dress.

—LIZ SMITH

"

The reason I talk to myself is that I'm the
only one whose answers I accept.

—GEORGE CARLIN

"

Spilling your guts is just exactly
as charming as it sounds.

—FRAN LEBOWITZ

"

As far as I'm concerned, "whom" is a word that was
invented to make everyone sound like a butler.

—CALVIN TRILLIN

"

Constantly talking isn't necessarily communicating.

—JIM CARREY

"

"Whining is anger through a small opening."

—AL FRANKEN

Health and Fitness, so to Speak

Cross-country skiing is great if you live in a small country.

—STEVEN WRIGHT

66

Whenever I feel like exercise, I lie down until the feeling passes.

—ROBERT HUTCHINS

66

I'm not a vegetarian because I love animals. I'm a vegetarian because I hate plants.

—A. WHITNEY BROWN

66

Housework can't kill you, but why take a chance?

—PHYLLIS DILLER

🐦 QUOTABLE TWEETS

A study found exercise may be bad for your health. Which means I'm not fat, I'm just morbidly over-healthed.

@StephenAtHome (Stephen Colbert)

THE PERFECT WORDS TO

Open with a Laugh

The human brain starts working the
moment you are born and never stops until
you stand up to speak in public.

—GEORGE JESSEL

"

A dead-end street is a good place to turn around.

—NAOMI JUDD

"

I've had a perfectly wonderful evening, but this wasn't it.

—GROUCHO MARX

"

The problem is never how to get new, innovative
thoughts into your mind, but how to get old ones out.

—DEE HOCK

"

It doesn't work to leap a twenty-foot
chasm in two ten-foot jumps.

—PROVERB

"

Great ideas often receive violent
opposition from mediocre minds.

—ALBERT EINSTEIN

A healthy male adult bore consumes
each year one and a half times his own
weight in other people's patience.

—JOHN UPDIKE

“

I have never taken any exercise except
sleeping and resting.

—MARK TWAIN

Yum!

....

Milk without fat is like nonalcoholic Scotch.

—ANDY ROONEY

“

You've got bad eating habits if you use
a grocery cart in a 7-Eleven, OK?

—DENNIS MILLER

“

Food, love, mother and career:
the four basic guilt groups.

—CATHY GUISEWITE

“

I don't share blame. I don't share credit.
And I don't share desserts.

—BEVERLY SILLS

"Turn your wounds into wisdom."

—OPRAH

WISEST WORDS

The insights of the greatest minds lead us to a deeper understanding of the world, humankind, and ourselves. Through the eyes of others we see new angles that can shape our own vision.

Wisdom

Wisdom outweighs any wealth.

—SOPHOCLES

"

There is a plan to this universe. There is
a high intelligence, maybe even a purpose, but
it's given to us on the installment plan.

—ISAAC BASHEVIS SINGER

"

Common sense is not so common.

—VOLTAIRE

"

I not only use all the brains that I have,
but all that I can borrow.

—WOODROW WILSON

"

To understand a new idea, break an old habit.

—JEAN TOOMER

"

Common sense is wisdom with its sleeves rolled up.

—KYLE FARNSWORTH

"

We use 10% of our brains. Imagine how much we
could accomplish if we used the other 60%.

—ELLEN DEGENERES

True wisdom has a curious way of revealing
to yourself your own true ignorance.

@neiltyson (Neil DeGrasse Tyson)

The man who complains about the way the ball
bounces is likely the one who dropped it.

—KENT HILL

"

You'll never have any mental muscle if you
don't have any heavy stuff to pick up.

—DIANE LANE

"

Turn your face to the sun and the
shadows fall behind you.

—JAN GOLDSTEIN

"

Never ask the barber if you need a haircut.

—WARREN BUFFETT

"

Be open to learning new lessons even if they
contradict the lessons you learned yesterday.

—ELLEN DEGENERES

Life

Think of life as a terminal illness, because
if you do, you will live it with joy and
passion, as it ought to be lived.

—ANNA QUINDLEN

"

There are only two ways to live your life.
One is as though nothing is a miracle. The other
is as though everything is a miracle.

—ALBERT EINSTEIN

"

There are no regrets in life, just lessons.

—JENNIFER ANISTON

"

If you're quiet, you're not living. You've got to be noisy
and colorful and lively.

—MEL BROOKS

"

The first step to getting the things you want out of life
is this: Decide what you want.

—BEN STEIN

"

Big changes in our lives are more or less
a second chance.

—HARRISON FORD

Find a spot on Earth that is comfortable for you.
Keep that spot clean physically or in your mind.
Think about the spot when you are away.

@yokoono

You don't have to have been near death to know . . .
what living is all about—but maybe it helps.

—LANCE ARMSTRONG

"

Life's a roller coaster, and you never know
when it's going to take a turn.

—TY PENNINGTON

"

Life is a series of commas, not periods.

—MATTHEW MCCONAUGHEY

"

Keep moving if you love life, and keep
your troubles well behind you.

—JOHN MCCAIN

"

I don't make plans, because life is short and
unpredictable—much like the weather!

—AL ROKER

Life's like a novel with the end ripped out.

—RASCAL FLATTS

"

Life is improvisation.

—TINA FEY

"

It isn't life that weighs us down—
it's the way we carry it.

—ELIZABETH POTIER

Truth

Truth may be stranger than fiction, goes the
old saw, but it is never as strange as lies.

—JOHN HODGMAN

"

The truth needs so little rehearsal.

—BARBARA KINGSOLVER

"

Delete the adjectives and [you'll] have the facts.

—HARPER LEE

"

Bad taste is simply saying the truth before
it should be said.

—MEL BROOKS

If you tell the truth, you don't need a long memory.

—JESSE VENTURA

"

The pursuit of truth is like picking raspberries.
You miss a lot if you approach it from only one angle.

—RANDAL MARLIN

"

Lying makes a problem part of the future;
truth makes a problem part of the past.

—RICK PITINO

Kindness

Do your little bit of good where you are; it is those little
bits of good put together that overwhelm the world.

—DESMOND TUTU

"

You cannot do a kindness too soon, for you never
know how soon it will be too late.

—RALPH WALDO EMERSON

"

A little kindness from person to person is
better than a vast love for all humankind.

—RICHARD DEHMEL

🐦 QUOTABLE TWEETS

Every mental event has a neural correlate.
Through mindfulness we can rewire the brain
for peace, harmony, laughter, and love.

@DeepakChopra

Whenever you see darkness, there is extraordinary
opportunity for the light to burn brighter.

—BONO

66

The everyday kindness of the back roads more than
makes up for the acts of greed in the headlines.

—CHARLES KURALT

66

Resolve to be tender with the young, compassionate
with the aged, sympathetic with the striving,
and tolerant with the weak and the wrong. Sometime
in life you will have been all of these.

—BOB GODDARD

66

Life is short and we never have enough time for
gladdening the hearts of those who travel the way
with us. Oh, be swift to love! Make haste to be kind.

—HENRI FRÉDÉRIC AMIEL

> "I have witnessed the softening of the hardest of hearts by a simple smile."
>
> —GOLDIE HAWN

If you can't be kind,
at least be vague.

—JUDITH MARTIN

❝

Ask any decent person what he thinks
matters most in human conduct: five to one
his answer will be "kindness."

—KENNETH CLARK

❝

How sweet it is when the strong are also gentle!

—LIBBIE FUDIM

❝

Kindness is never wasted. If it has no effect on
the recipient, at least it benefits the bestower.

—S. H. SIMMONS

Two important things are to have a genuine interest in people and to be kind to them. Kindness, I've discovered, is everything in life.

—ISAAC BASHEVIS SINGER

"

Always try to be a little kinder than is necessary.

—JAMES M. BARRIE

"

Kindness is more important than wisdom, and the recognition of this is the beginning of wisdom.

—THEODORE ISAAC RUBIN, MD

Giving & Gratitude

There are three words I like to repeat to myself: glass half full. Just to remind myself to be grateful for everything I have.

—GOLDIE HAWN

"

Giving never happens by accident.
It's always intentional.

—AMY GRANT

"

True giving happens when we give from our heart.

—MUHAMMAD ALI

If you give everybody a slice of pie, you
will still have more than enough.

—JAY LENO

"

Be thankful for what you have—
you'll end up having more.

—OPRAH

"

I challenge anybody in their darkest moment to write
what they're grateful for, even stupid little things like
green grass or a friendly conversation with somebody
on the elevator. You start to realize how rich you are.

—JIM CARREY

"

Outcomes rarely turn on grand gestures
or the art of the deal, but on whether you've
sent someone a thank-you note.

—BERNIE BRILLSTEIN

THE PERFECT WORDS FOR
Pep Talks

It's a shallow life that doesn't give a person a few scars.
—GARRISON KEILLOR

"

If you are not criticized, you may not be doing much.
—DONALD RUMSFELD

"

He who limps is still walking.
—STANISLAW LEC

"

He who cannot forgive others destroys the bridge
over which he himself must pass.
—GEORGE HERBERT

"

What does not kill him, makes him stronger.
—FRIEDRICH NIETZSCHE

"

Write injuries in sand, kindnesses in marble.
—FRENCH PROVERB

"

If we were born knowing everything, what would
we do with all this time on this earth?
—NELLY

Character

If you don't have enemies, you don't have character.

—PAUL NEWMAN

"

Character—the willingness to accept
responsibility for one's own life—is the source
from which self-respect springs.

—JOAN DIDION

"

Great acting is being able to create a character.
Great character is being able to be yourself.

—JOHN LEGUIZAMO

"

You grow up the day you have your first
real laugh—at yourself.

—ETHEL BARRYMORE

"

Tension is who you think you should be.
Relaxation is who you are.

—CHINESE PROVERB

"

The greatest conflicts are not between two people
but between one person and himself.

—GARTH BROOKS

"When you finally accept that you're a complete dork, your life gets easier. No sense in trying to be cool."

—REESE WITHERSPOON

A man who builds his own pedestal had better use strong cement.

—ANNA QUINDLEN

"

The more I like me, the less I want to pretend to be other people.

—JAMIE LEE CURTIS

"

When wealth is lost, nothing is lost. When health is lost, something is lost. When character is lost, all is lost.

—REV. BILLY GRAHAM

The true measure of a man is how he treats someone
who can do him absolutely no good.

—ANN LANDERS

"

I've never believed in measuring one's worth
by the size of his or her bank account. I prefer
to look at distance traveled.

—DAN RATHER

"

It ain't what people call you. It's what you answer to.

—TYLER PERRY

Forgiveness

Never does the human soul appear so
strong and noble as when it forgoes revenge
and dares to forgive an injury.

—E. H. CHAPIN

"

One of the most lasting pleasures you can experience
is the feeling that comes over you when you genuinely
forgive an enemy—whether he knows it or not.

—O. A. BATTISTA

QUOTABLE TWEETS

Forgiveness is not a feeling; it is a commitment.

@DrGaryChapman

When a deep injury is done us, we never recover until we forgive.

—ALAN PATON

"

Forgiveness is a gift of high value. Yet its cost is nothing.

—BETTY SMITH

"

A forgiveness ought to be like a canceled note, torn in two and burned up, so that it can never be shown against the man.

—HENRY WARD BEECHER

"

Forgive your enemies—if you can't get back at them any other way.

—FRANKLIN P. JONES

"

Forgiveness is a funny thing. It warms the heart and cools the sting.

—WILLIAM ARTHUR WARD

206

One of the secrets of a long and fruitful
life is to forgive everybody everything
every night before you go to bed.

—ANN LANDERS

66

Forgiving and being forgiven are two
names for the same thing. The important thing
is that a discord has been resolved.

—C. S. LEWIS

Dreams

Dreams come true; without that possibility,
nature would not incite us to have them.

—JOHN UPDIKE

66

The mind is the limit. As long as the mind
can envision something, you can do it.

—ARNOLD SCHWARZENEGGER

66

If your world doesn't allow you to dream,
move to one where you can.

—BILLY IDOL

THE PERFECT WORDS FOR
Life-Changing Advice

The most important trip you may take in life
is meeting people halfway.

—HENRY BOYE

"

It takes no more time to see the good
side of life than to see the bad.

—JIMMY BUFFETT

"

The squeaky wheel may get the most oil,
but it's also the first to be replaced.

—MARILYN VOS SAVANT

"

Never tell anyone to go to hell
unless you can make 'em go.

—BILL CLINTON

"

Live every day like it's your last,
'cause one day you're gonna be right.

—RAY CHARLES

"

Hunches are not to be sneezed at.

—RICHARD NELSON BOLLES

If you believe you have a foolproof system you have
failed to take into consideration the creativity of fools.

—FRANK W. ABAGNALE

"

Learn to enjoy your own company.
You are the one person you can count on
living with for the rest of your life.

—ANN RICHARDS

"

One trouble with trouble is that it
usually starts out like fun.

—ANN LANDERS

"

If you don't get out of the box you've been raised in,
you won't understand how much bigger the world is.

—ANGELINA JOLIE

"

Kindness consists in loving people more
than they deserve.

—JOSEPH JOUBERT

"

An eye for an eye only leads to more blindness.

—MARGARET ATWOOD

It's better to look at the sky than live there.
Such an empty place; so vague. Just a country
where the thunder goes and things disappear.

—TRUMAN CAPOTE

"

All our dreams can come true—
if we have the courage to pursue them.

—WALT DISNEY

Intentions

The smallest deed is greater than
the grandest intention.

—PATTI LABELLE

"

Good intentions are not enough. They've never
put an onion in the soup yet.

—SONYA LEVIEN

"

People judge you by your actions,
not your intentions. You may have a heart
of gold, but so has a hard-boiled egg.

—*GOOD READING*

A man who wants to do something will find a way;
a man who doesn't will find an excuse.

—STEPHEN DOLLEY, JR.

"

You can't build a reputation on what you are going to do.

—HENRY FORD

Responsibility

Few things help an individual more than
to place responsibility upon him and to
let him know that you trust him.

—BOOKER T. WASHINGTON

"

Responsible, who wants to be responsible?
Whenever something bad happens it's always,
who's responsible for this?

—JERRY SEINFELD

If you read someone else's diary,
you get what you deserve.

—DAVID SEDARIS

"

No snowflake in an avalanche ever feels responsible.

—STANISLAW LEC

"

To say my fate is not tied to your fate is like
saying, "Your end of the boat is sinking."

—HUGH DOWNS

"

The willingness to accept responsibility for one's own
life is the source from which self-respect springs.

—JOAN DIDION

"

Most of us can read the writing on the wall;
we just assume it's addressed to someone else.

—IVERN BALL

Yes & No

A "No" uttered from the deepest conviction
is better than a "Yes" merely uttered to
please, or worse, to avoid trouble.

—MAHATMA GANDHI

Saying no to something is actually much
more powerful than saying yes.

—TOM HANKS

❝

I live by the truth that "No" is a complete sentence.

—ANNE LAMOTT

❝

Cynics always say no. Saying yes leads to knowledge.
So for as long as you have the strength to, say yes.

—STEPHEN COLBERT

❝

Learn to say "no" to the good so you
can say "yes" to the best.

—JOHN C. MAXWELL

❝

Yes and *No* are very short words to say, but we should
think for some length of time before saying them.

—UNKNOWN

Anger

....

Temper is the one thing you can't
get rid of by losing it.

—JACK NICHOLSON

213

Keep Calm & Carry On

God, grant me the serenity to accept the things
I cannot change, the courage to change the things
I can, and the wisdom to know the difference.

—REINHOLD NIEBUHR

"

The quieter you become, the more you can hear.

—RAM DASS

"

Be master of mind rather than mastered by mind.

—ZEN PROVERB

"

A crust eaten in peace is better than
a banquet partaken in anxiety.

—AESOP

"

Take a deep breath and don't take
any of it too seriously.

—CHER

"

Your mind will answer most questions if you
learn to relax and wait for the answer.

—WILLIAM S. BURROUGHS

Nothing is permanent in this wicked world.
Not even our troubles.

—CHARLIE CHAPLIN

"

Slow down and everything you are chasing
will come around and catch you.

—JOHN DE PAOLA

"

I took a deep breath and listened to the
old bray of my heart. I am. I am. I am.

—SYLVIA PLATH

"

We shall not flag nor fail.
We shall go on to the end.

—WINSTON CHURCHILL

"

Serenity now!

—FRANK COSTANZA (ON *SEINFELD*)

"

Sitting quietly, doing nothing, spring comes,
and the grass grows by itself.

—*ZENRIN*

"I never liked anyone who didn't have
a temper. If you don't have any temper,
you don't have any passion."
—MICHAEL BLOOMBERG

"

Anger must be the energy that has not
yet found its right channel.
—FLORIDA SCOTT-MAXWELL

"

Never harbor grudges; they sour
your stomach
and do no harm to anyone else.
—ROBERTSON DAVIES

"

It would be great if people never got
angry at someone for doing something
they've done themselves.
—RODNEY DANGERFIELD

"

You don't have good grammar when
you type with your fists.
—C.F. PAYNE

Death & Dying

When I was sick, I didn't want to die. When I race, I don't want to lose. Dying and losing, it's the same thing.

—LANCE ARMSTRONG

❝

I'm always relieved when someone delivers a eulogy and I realize I'm listening to it.

—GEORGE CARLIN

❝

The fear of death follows from the fear of life. A man who lives fully is prepared to die at any time.

—MARK TWAIN

❝

I don't want to achieve immortality through my work. I want to achieve immortality through not dying.

—WOODY ALLEN

INDEX

Also Available
from Reader's Digest

Laughter, the Best Medicine @Work

Lighten up and laugh your way through the 9-to-5 grind with this mix of hilarious wisecracks, uproarious one-liners, full-color cartoons, and quotations from famous (and not-so-famous) wits. Whether you suffer from an e-mail gone wrong, an irritating coworker, or a dreadful boss, you'll see that laughter *is* the best medicine for all your work woes.

ISBN 978-1-60652-479-4 • $9.99 paperback

13 Things They Won't Tell You

From the wildly popular *Reader's Digest* column "13 Things," this book features more than 1,000 trade secrets for living smarter, richer, and happier. We asked hundreds of professionals in dozens of fields: What are the things you wish people knew? What should they know? What do you think they would be shocked to know? You won't believe what they said!

ISBN 978-1-60652-499-2 • $19.99 hardcover

Now *That's* Funny!

What do you get when you cross America's favorite magazine with the life work of an unapologetic joke thief? This book! In this rollicking collection, humor editor Andy Simmons has gathered the funniest jokes, interviews, essays, and anecdotes from the pages of *Reader's Digest* magazine, the oddest corner's of the country, and his own life.

ISBN 978-1-60652-500-5 • $14.99 paperback

The Best Life Stories

When *Reader's Digest* invited readers to "share a lesson, simple advice, a funny moment, or other story from your life," more than 6,500 people submitted entries. Of those, 150 were carefully selected for this collection. These stories reveal the uncommon wit and wisdom of ordinary people who look at life in extraordinary ways. From poetic to prosaic, heartwrenching to humorous, *The Best Life Stories* proves that every one of us learns lessons worth sharing in our day-to-day struggles, joys, and triumphs.

ISBN 978-1-60652-564-7 • $12.99 hardcover

For more information, visit us at RDTradePublishing.com
E-book editions are also available.
Reader's Digest books can be purchased through retail and online bookstores.
In the United States books are distributed by Penguin Group (USA) Inc.
For more information or to order books, call 1-800-788-6262.